The Sabbath Experiment

The Sabbath Experiment

Spiritual Formation
for Living in a Non-Stop World

ROB MUTHIAH

CASCADE *Books* · Eugene, Oregon

THE SABBATH EXPERIMENT
Spiritual Formation for Living in a Non-Stop World

Cascade Books
An Imprint of Wipf and Stock Publishers
199 W. 8th Ave., Suite 3
Eugene, OR 97401

www.wipfandstock.com

ISBN 13: 978-1-4982-2419-2

Cataloging-in-Publication data:

Muthiah, Robert A.

The Sabbath experiment : spiritual formation for living in a non-stop world / Rob Muthiah.

xii + 106 p. ; 23 cm. —Includes bibliographical references.

ISBN 13: 978-1-4982-2419-2

1. Sabbath. 2. Spiritual formation. 3. Spiritual life—Christianity. I. Title.

BV4501.3 M87 2015

Manufactured in the U.S.A.

To Lionel and Marion Muthiah

CONTENTS

PREFACE

During my years of involvement in seminary education, first as a student and later as a professor, I have seen a shift in relation to spiritual formation. For a while, it seemed that every book and article about seminary education critiqued seminaries for teaching esoteric theology while ignoring their students' spiritual formation. Seminaries took note, and in recent years more and more seminaries have been intentional about structuring spiritual formation into their programs.

In my own teaching as a seminary faculty member, one of the approaches to spiritual formation that I have found most powerful for students is that of Sabbath keeping. The practice is so rich theologically that it constantly opens new horizons of understanding for these theologically curious and questioning minds. The practice is intriguing because it is ancient and yet new to many of my students. And here's the important part: my students find that the practice of keeping the Sabbath actually does something—it forms them spiritually in profound ways.

My hope in writing this book is that this approach to spiritual formation might ripple out to other parts of the church—and there are many—that have lost the ancient skill of practicing Sabbath. I have three audiences in mind as I write. First, I have in mind those of you who consider yourselves ordinary, faithful members of local churches. Perhaps you are a landscaper, a teacher, a business executive, or a stay-at-home parent. I want you to know and experience that Sabbath is possible and life-giving, even (or, especially) in today's culture. I try to take seriously your realities of juggling work, parenting, church involvement, recreation, and all the other things in your lives as I invite you to Sabbath.

Second, I have in mind those of you who are pastors. You are notorious for not taking care of yourselves! I wonder if you might re-claim Sabbath as a way of tending to your own spirits—for God's sake, for the sake of yourselves, and for the sake of those you serve in your churches. Additionally, my hope is that you will draw on ideas included in this book as you thoughtfully attend to the spiritual formation of your flock. Pastors face a unique challenge in relation to Sabbath: what does Sabbath look like for pastors when Sunday morning preaching and leadership responsibilities are part of their job descriptions? I've included some creative approaches that some pastors have used related to this issue (see chapter 2, "Sabbath, Rest, and Work").

Third, I have in mind those of you who are seminary and college students interested in the life of the church, a group of folks dear to my heart. If you are a student reading this, it has probably been assigned for a class (I am well aware that students seldom have time to read anything else!). My hope is that the theology and practice of Sabbath will contribute to your spiritual formation during this season of focused study in your lives and that what you learn and practice now will sustain you long after your degree programs are completed.

I will weave together three approaches in this book. One approach is to look at the theology of Sabbath that emerges from Scripture. No, I'm not going to try to get us to follow all the detailed Sabbath practices described in the Old Testament (I certainly won't be promoting the instruction to stone those who *don't* keep Sabbath, found in Numbers 15:35!). However, by probing the teachings on Sabbath contained in both the Old and New Testaments, we'll gain insight into the theological dimensions that are still present in our Sabbath keeping today.

A second approach I will use is to look at how Sabbath relates to some of the forces at work in the dominant culture today, forces such as individualism, consumerism, and technology. This could easily devolve into a simplistic "Christianity vs. the dominant culture" rant—good vs. evil. But for us as Christians, to wrestle with how we should relate to our host culture in a given time and place is more complex than that. Sabbath forms us into a contrast community, but Sabbath also sends us back into the dominant culture to engage, to love, and to join in God's transforming work in this world. We'll look at ways in which that might happen.

Third, I will tell stories of how various people are living out this practice today, give concrete suggestions for Sabbath observance, and point to some of the challenges of observing the Sabbath in our fast-paced, post-Christian culture. The goal here is to move from ideas about Sabbath to actually living out Sabbath practices in the rhythm of our weeks.

Whether you read this book on your own or as part of a group, keep in mind that Sabbath always has a communal element. I point to this numerous times throughout this book. You will get the most out of this book if you approach it communally; find others with whom to discuss the questions provided at the end of each chapter.

I number the Sabbath commandment as the fourth commandment in this book, but I am aware that some traditions place it at number three. See the call-out box on page 26 for a comparison of these numbering systems.

Throughout this book, when I refer to the Sabbath Experiment, I'm referring to a twenty-four hour experience that I give to my students as a class assignment. You will be invited to try the experiment, too. Call-out boxes throughout this book with the title "Reflecting on the Sabbath Experiment" contain quotations (used with permission) from students' papers in which they reflect on their Sabbath Experiment. The guidelines for the Sabbath Experiment are included in Appendix 2, and at the end of chapter six you will be invited to carry out the experiment yourself.

Between each chapter you will find short "Slowing Down" sections. Each "Slowing Down" section provides a chance to slow down for a moment from the main narrative of the book and to go deeper with a portion of Scripture related to Sabbath. If you are using this book with a discussion group, each of these sections could be given its own week for discussion or combined with the chapter that comes before it.

As you step into this exploration of Sabbath, may you come to know more fully the mysteries of Sabbath and may you drink deeply from its refreshing, still waters.

Rob Muthiah
Easter, 2015

one

SABBATH AS GIFT
Living Well in a 25/8 Culture

I was driving the carpool home from our daughter's high school one afternoon when I heard one of the teenagers in the car use the phrase "25/8." I hadn't heard that phrase before, but the context quickly revealed its meaning. We all know the phrase 24/7, but now there's a concept of time *beyond* 24/7 that has entered the lingo of our culture: 25/8! It's an amount of time we cannot actually live in, a pace of life that passes us by, a rush of demands and information that leaves us struggling impossibly to keep up. It signifies a frenzied culture that cares little for human limits or human thriving. It's a social force that overwhelms, suffocates, crushes. It captures a feeling that many people today live with, a feeling of not being able to keep up with life, a feeling of drowning in the demands of life.

What if someone offered you a guaranteed way to fix all this, to eliminate worry and stress from your life, to feel fully rested, to connect deeply with God and with others in this age of technological frenzy, to be swept up in joy and celebration, to fight injustice, and to care for creation? Would you sign up? Take the pill? Drink the medicinal tea? Watch the video? Join the class? Buy the book?

Alright. I'm not offering Sabbath as a cure-all or a new gospel of salvation. It's not a magic pill or a secret elixir. But I'm not going to back off too far. A Sabbath way of living offers a dramatic alternative to the 25/8 whirlwind, and it will change your life profoundly if you let it. In a culture that entices us to worship at the altars of shopping, image creation, and the latest and greatest tech gadgets, Sabbath confronts these gods by rooting us in joyful worship of our triune God. In a culture that strains and fragments our relationships and communities, Sabbath provides a way of experiencing wholeness and integration. In an age when human trafficking and environmental degradation are rampant, Sabbath keeping reveals to us the social justice and earth care dimensions of Christian discipleship. In a time of cynicism and despair, Sabbath leads us into delight and hope. This ancient practice is a gift for our time.

These are lofty claims. Can Sabbath really live up to them? I invite you to evaluate these claims for yourself as you examine them more closely. But to do so, you will need to do more than read about Sabbath. The truthfulness of these claims can only be tested by practicing Sabbath. This reality is captured in a story passed along by Samuel Dresner:

> The Roman Emperor Hadrian asked Rabbi Joshua ben Hananiah, "Why is it that Sabbath foods have such a fragrant scent?"
>
> Rabbi Joshua answered, "We put in a certain spice called Sabbath."
>
> The Emperor said, "Please give me some of that spice."
>
> Rabbi Joshua answered, "It can only be tasted by those who keep the Sabbath."[1]

If you want to taste Sabbath to see if indeed this gift is good, you will need to *keep* the Sabbath, not just agree with ideas *about* the Sabbath. This is the journey to which I invite you. Ponder the ideas set forth in this book, dwell on the Scripture passages related to Sabbath, and try adding some of the suggested Sabbath elements to your Sundays over the weeks and months ahead. *Then* ask yourself and those who join you in the practice whether these lofty claims hold up.

Some of you may already be faithfully living into this practice. For you, I hope this book provides renewal and deepens your understanding of the purposes for Sabbath observance. For others, to embrace Sabbath will involve baby steps further along the path of observance or tweaks to current patterns. For yet others, a move to embrace Sabbath will be much more difficult or dramatic, a rebirth into an astonishingly different way of seeing and living in this world. Regardless of your path, I trust that Christ will meet you along the way and bless your efforts.

---

1. Dresner, *Sabbath*, 21–22.

The Sabbath Bride

Often conversations about Sabbath quickly bend toward questions about what we can or can't do on Sunday: Can I garden? Can I go for a run? Can I watch football? I don't mean to discount these questions (and I'll address them later), but to understand the meaning of Sabbath we must start somewhere else: by focusing on the *spirit* of the Sabbath. As we seek to embrace the joyful, grace-filled spirit of Sabbath, we can learn from the Jewish tradition's image of the day as the Sabbath Bride (*Shabbat HaKallah*).[2]

The tradition holds that just as those gathered for a wedding wait with excitement for the arrival of the bride, so too are we to anticipate the arrival of the Sabbath Bride. And the tradition suggests that just as the gathered family and friends are filled with joy and a spirit of celebration when the bride finally arrives, so too are we to orient our hearts toward joy and celebration in the presence of the Sabbath Bride. Finally, the tradition points to the departure of the bride, when those gathered for the wedding feel an afterglow of delight and satisfaction from their time in her presence, and a longing for the next time they will see her. The afterglow and longing for the bride to come again are the feelings that the departure of the Sabbath Bride should elicit in us.

The metaphor of the Sabbath Bride is deeply meaningful because it captures the spirit of Sabbath. In contrast, the idea of keeping the Sabbath has often been framed as dour, boring, and oppressive. Puritan perspectives on the Sabbath, mediated for some of us through nineteenth-century stories such as *The Adventures of Huckleberry Finn* and the *Little House on the Prairie* series, saw the day as a day for wearing uncomfortable clothing and for sitting still without smiling, laughing, or playing. It was a day filled with boredom, which one endured as a sign of faithfulness. It was a day that everyone—especially kids—was eager to see come to an end.

The Sabbath Bride provides a dramatically different image from this Puritan-influenced view of Sabbath. The Sabbath Bride imagery is festive, not dull and boring. It moves us away from dour seriousness to a spirit of celebration. It helps us to see the day as a gift filled by God with delight and grace.

I'm a pretty good rule-follower, and sometimes that has its benefits. But in relation to Sabbath keeping, I can easily get wrapped up in holding to rules or guidelines in a way that actually *inhibits* the arrival of the

---

2. Ibid., 16.

Sabbath Bride. For example, I love to have the house clean and in order for the start of Sabbath, which our family begins with our Saturday evening meal. The problem is that I can easily slip into the role of "household general" when it comes to these cleaning projects, and I bark orders at the kids about socks that are still on the living room floor, dirty dishes that didn't get put in the dishwasher, or school backpacks plopped down in the dining room. When I do this, I am creating an atmosphere of rules and control rather than one of anticipation and celebration. When my own spirit is not aligned with that of the Sabbath Bride, I do little to invite others into the joy of this set-apart time.

How are Christian Sabbath, the Lord's Day, and Sunday Related?

The first Jewish Christians continued to observe the Sabbath on the seventh day of the week. Soon after Jesus rose from the grave on the first day of the week, early Christians began to gather on the first day of each week also to celebrate the Resurrection and fellowship together. This was not initially a whole day set apart in the manner of the Jewish Sabbath. Rather, Christians would gather after work in the evening on this day, often in people's homes. And they came to call the day the Lord's Day, a reference to which is found in Rev 1:10.

As the fledgling church moved further and further from its Jewish roots, and as gathering on the Lord's Day became more widely spread among Christians, Sabbath observance on the seventh day of the week began to decline. Christians understood their freedom in Christ to include freedom from the laws of Sabbath (Col 2:16).

In the fourth century, Constantine declared each Sunday to be an official day off from work in the Roman empire. Though he had by this time publicly converted to Christianity, his edict regarding Sundays did not connect Sunday to the Lord's Day or any other aspect of Christianity. The edict did, however, allow Christians to now refrain from work on Sundays. It was left to Christians in subsequent years, most notably Augustine at the start of the fifth century, to solidify the melding of Sunday with Sabbath and to reclaim Sabbath practices for Christians.

A few denominations today continue the original pattern of observing Sabbath on the last day of the week, but most of the church has moved Sabbath to the first day of the week, Sunday. So through historical and theological development, the Sabbath, the Lord's Day, and Sunday have become one.

Here's another scenario. Our youngest son sometimes needs a reminder that we're choosing to fill our Sundays before church with things other than screen time. At times I've delivered the reminder with a heavy-handed, dictatorial or "gotcha" tone of voice, but in my better moments I do it gently and then invite him to do the Sunday newspaper's parent-child crossword puzzle with me or something of that sort. It seems to me that the first approach is likely to foster in our son—and myself—a rule-bound view of Sabbath, whereas the second approach is more likely to enable both of us to welcome the Sabbath Bride. And it is in the presence of the Sabbath Bride that we feel the gift of joy, delight, and laughter in this set-apart day.

In the Sabbath Experiment guidelines (see Appendix 2), the first assignment is to identify one thing you might include to help you celebrate on the Sabbath. Those who have done the Sabbath Experiment often choose things like inviting friends over for a meal, going for a walk, or listening to some favorite music. The intention of putting this guideline first in the experiment is to encourage a heart orientation that celebrates the Sabbath Bride. The other Sabbath Experiment guidelines give specific structure to the day, but the structure is only rightly understood in light of the spirit of the day.

> *Reflecting on the Sabbath Experiment:*
> **The Day as Gift**
>
> *"What was first interesting to me as my wife and I sat to discuss the Sabbath Experiment was my own negativity. I looked through the experiment with a red pen and started scratching out what I wasn't going to be able to do. My wife placed her hand on mine and said, 'Isn't the Sabbath a gift? Maybe we should pray and ask the Lord for a better attitude and ask him how we should approach this gift.' Urg, my heart sank. As we sat and prayed, I realized that my attitude was stinky and that God had a gift for me as I did this experiment."*
> — *Mike*
> *Executive Pastor*

The Jewish tradition has a song, called *L'khah Dodi*, that is sung in synagogues on Friday evening to welcome the presence of the Sabbath Bride. For most of the song the congregation faces forward toward the Ark, but when they reach the final verse, they turn toward the entrance and bow to symbolically welcome the day, and they sing these words directed toward the Sabbath Bride:

> Come in peace, and come in joy,
> Thou who art thy bridegroom's pride;
> Come, O bride, and shed thy grace

O'er the faithful chosen race;
Come, O bride! Come, O bride![3]

As we learn to welcome the Sabbath Bride, we orient ourselves toward the joy and the celebration that God intends to be part of this day of rest.

The Sabbath Queen

The Jewish tradition offers a second way of imagining this day with a metaphor that works in tandem with the Sabbath Bride: the tradition also characterizes the day as the Sabbath Queen (*Shabbat HaMalkah*).[4] What would you do if you knew a real live queen were coming to your home for a visit? I'd probably begin with cleaning and organizing—dust the furniture, sweep the floors, tidy up the various piles on the coffee table, scrub the bathroom, and clean out the refrigerator (not that the queen is going to be digging around for a soda or leftovers). I'd also want to prepare socially. What is the proper way to greet a queen—bow? Kiss her hand? Just wave awkwardly? And what do you talk about with a queen, or what do you *not* talk about? I'd want to know the protocols or expectations.

The Sabbath Queen is a way of conceptualizing the protocols of the day, a way of attending to the rhythms and practices we choose to put in place for the day. The Sabbath Queen relates to our outer behavioral expression of Sabbath. This means giving careful attention to how we prepare for the day and to what we do or don't do on this day. The Sabbath Queen brings structure and order to the day and expects subservience from her subjects—she expects those in her presence to obey her decree that all work should cease. Whereas the Sabbath Bride elicits warm emotions, the Sabbath Queen transcends emotions or moods. As Dresner says:

> A [person's] mood, be it ever so ennobling, ever so profound, ever so praiseworthy, is frail, transient, open to change and transmutation. The Queen comes to prevent such change, to guarantee the mood, to lend stability and permanence to what might otherwise fly away.[5]

While they sound different notes, the Sabbath Queen and the Sabbath Bride harmonize beautifully. On the one hand, the spirit of the day

3. Ibid., 19.

4. Ibid., 20.

5. Ibid., 25.

(the Bride) cannot be sustained without giving the day some structure (the Queen). On the other hand, if we get too caught up in the behavior or structure of the day, the spirit of Sabbath becomes muted or drowned out completely. We need both the Sabbath Bride *and* the Sabbath Queen in order to hear the fullness of the Sabbath symphony. Dresner describes the relationship between the two like this:

> If *Kallah*, or Bride, is the symbol of love, *Malkah*, or Queen, is the symbol of law; if *Kallah* evokes devotion, *Malkah* demands obedi-ence; if *Kallah* stands for feeling, *Malkah* represents observance. Inwardness, important though it may be, is not enough. There must likewise be an outward form, a pattern of conduct, a definite way.
>
> Indeed, one can never truly know the inward feeling of the Sabbath without the outward form.[6]

Dresner goes on to describe why the Bride and the Queen need each other:

> The love of the *Kallah* without the law of the *Malkah* would quick-ly fall to pieces and disintegrate; it would have no substance, no reality, no pattern for expression, no protection, no guarantee of permanence. On the other hand, the law of the *Malkah* without the love of the *Kallah* would mean a harsh, officious, legalistic day, a time of gloom and restriction and rebellion.[7]

I am by personality more naturally inclined toward the Sabbath Queen. I most readily focus on the structure of the day. I can be scrupulous about not making lists (something the rabbinic tradition rules out on the Sabbath), because doing so turns my attention towards things that need to be accomplished. And the Sabbath is in part about leaving aside our compulsions to accomplish things. I can be rigidly committed to not buy-ing anything on this one day of the week as a way of resisting the claims of the marketplace on my life and protesting the injustices that come with our economic system. But I am in constant need of embracing and re-embrac-ing the *spirit* of the day, the Sabbath Bride. I am prone to seek control over the day, which of course is ironic given that the day is supposed to highlight the fact that *God* is the one who has ultimate control, and I control so much less than I think I do. Over and over again, I must ask myself: Where is the

---

6. Ibid., 21.

7. Ibid., 25–26.

joy? Where is the grace? Am I receiving the day as gift? Of the Bride and the Queen, I myself am most in need of opening to the Sabbath Bride.

Others have a different challenge. They find it easy to relax, to enjoy non-compulsive moments, to laugh, to tell stories, to marvel at the beauty all around . . . at least on those rare occasions when life slows down enough for such moments to appear. I frequently talk to people who wistfully express a desire for this sort of Sabbath experience, but find that it rarely appears. Their challenge is not the difficulty of embracing the emotional posture of Sabbath; their challenge is being disciplined to put structure in place that creates time for Sabbath.

Some people chafe at structure, desiring to simply stay open to what might spontaneously happen. But Sabbath doesn't just happen. We must prepare for it. There is room within this set-aside day for spontaneity, but the day must be set aside, and that takes planning. It won't force itself upon us. We must "make Sabbath," to use a phrase from the Jewish tradition.[8] If you find it challenging to plan how you will structure the day, perhaps the path forward for you involves acknowledging the Sabbath Queen.

The Sabbath Bride and the Sabbath Queen collaborate to achieve Sabbath rest (*Shabbat Menuhah*).[9] This is the landing place. This rest is what the planning and thoughtfulness move us toward. This is the rest we have when our workday activities and thoughts are set aside. It is more, though, than just a stopping of our work. As Abraham Joshua Heschel puts it,

> *Menuha* which we usually render with "rest" means here much more than withdrawal from labor and exertion, more than freedom from toil, strain or activity of any kind. *Menuha* is not a negative concept but something real and intrinsically positive . . . .
>
> To the biblical mind *menuha* is the same as happiness and stillness, as peace and harmony. . . . It is the state in which there is no strife and no fighting, no fear and no distrust. The essence of the good life is *menuha*.[10]

As we seek to understand Sabbath rest, Heschel's words invite us to consider not only what this rest *excludes* or what it is *not*, but also to consider what Sabbath rest *includes* or what it *is*. In the chapters ahead we take up that invitation. As we explore the many dimensions of Sabbath, I hope you will come to see and experience the profound beauty of this priceless

---

8. Ibid., 23.

9. Ibid., 26.

10. Heschel, *Sabbath*, 22–23.

gift. I offer the following story as an invitation to unwrap and marvel at this gift.

Somewhere in the Dingzhou prefecture of northern China during the tenth or eleventh century, a skilled craftsman delicately carved designs into a clay bowl and placed it in a kiln. The ceramics that emerged from this kiln were no ordinary objects. Known as Ding ceramics, they were exquisite works of art, whitish in color, created for the imperial court and wealthy merchants of the Song Dynasty. One of these stunning Ding bowls made a remarkable journey.

We're not sure of its full route, but perhaps the bowl was handed down for several generations in China before being given as a gift to a visiting ambassador from a far off land. Perhaps upon the death of this dignitary, his estate was divided between his several children, and then divided again and again for a few more generations until the origin of the handed-down bowl was long forgotten, though its beauty remained. And perhaps a descendent of that ambassador carefully packed up this bowl and brought it with her to the New World, where it was eventually forgotten in a box in an attic.

We can only speculate about most of the bowl's thousand-year journey, but we know the real story of the bowl starting in 2007. In that year, a family in New York went to a local rummage sale where they paid three dollars for an attractive five-inch bowl. They took it home and displayed it on their mantle. Six years later, someone suggested that they find out more about the bowl, and to their amazement, they discovered that they had an extremely rare Ding bowl; only one other like it is known to exist worldwide. In 2013, this Ding bowl sold at a Sotheby's auction for 2.2 million dollars. Even such an extravagant sum does not adequately capture the bowl's beauty and value.

For decades or even centuries, the value of this bowl had gone unrecognized. But through the thousand years since it emerged from the kiln, the bowl retained its beauty and often waited to be re-discovered.

So it is with Sabbath. For centuries, this ancient gift has been valued by some generations and lost by others, re-discovered by some, then forgotten in a box in a dusty attic, awaiting re-discovery so that we might experience again its exquisite beauty. If Sabbath has been lost in your household or community of believers, my hope is that you will re-discover this gift, a rhythm of life set in place by our generous, loving, and gracious God. This is the God who in Sabbath rest receives our worship and offers us the most abundant life possible, a life rooted in God's creation, a life redeemed and transformed by the saving work of Christ, and a life filled with the Spirit who leads us forward into God's preferred future. It is a future we taste each week when we enter Sabbath time.

Discussion Questions

1. What has been your understanding of Sabbath, and how has that shifted (if at all) over the years?

2. Which are you more drawn to: the Sabbath Bride or the Sabbath Queen? Which are you most in need of at this point in your life?

3. Most Christians already embrace the Sabbath practice of worshipping together on Sunday. Do you currently have other elements that are part of your Sabbath observance?

4. What activities might you add to your Sabbath observance to help you *celebrate* the day?

5. What are the cultural norms regarding Sabbath keeping in your church, city, region, or country?

↱ SLOWING DOWN
Grounding the Fourth Commandment Theologically

Scripture contains two primary versions of the Ten Commandments. One list is found in Exod 20:1–17 and a second list is found in Deut 5:6–21. While the commandments are the same in both places, some differences exist in the way they are described, especially when it comes to the Sabbath commandment. These differences combine to provide a rich theological grounding for Sabbath. As the story of God's people unfolds, the theology of Sabbath continues to morph and expand in Scripture, but it is grounded first in these two places. Let's take a look.

The Sabbath commandment in Exodus recalls that in the creation event God rested on the seventh day: "The Lord made the heavens and the earth, the sea, and everything that is in them in six days, but rested on the seventh day. That is why the Lord blessed the Sabbath day and made it holy" (Exod 20:11).[1] The Israelites were to imitate God by modeling the rhythm of their week after the rhythm created by God in the beginning of time. In Exodus, the Sabbath commandment is grounded in the order of creation.

In Deuteronomy, rather than being grounded in the order of creation, the Sabbath commandment is grounded in the order of redemption. In observing it, the Israelites are to recall that God delivered them out of Egypt: "Remember that you were a slave in Egypt, but the Lord your God brought you out of there with a strong hand and an outstretched arm. That's why the Lord your God commands you to keep the Sabbath day" (Deut 5:15). You were slaves and God delivered you—never forget that! The freedom to observe Sabbath results from God's work of deliverance. In Deuteronomy, the Sabbath commandment is grounded in the order of redemption.

Another interesting difference between these two versions of the commandment is how they begin. Both versions begin with an action word, but the word differs between them. The opening action word in Exodus is tied to memory: "Remember the Sabbath day and treat it as holy" (Exod 20:8). Remember. This kind of remembering is like remembering a wedding

---

1. All scripture quotations are from the Common English Bible unless otherwise noted.

11

anniversary—it involves remembering to do certain things on that day, but it also involves remembering the years that have led up to this anniversary and all that they have held. So in remembering to do or not do certain things on the Sabbath, the Israelites would also remember that they serve the Lord of the universe who brought everything into being at the beginning of time. And they would remember all the ways God had been faithful and cared for them through the ups and downs of their history. Remember. Cease work and be reminded that your Lord God made the heavens and the earth. As an act of remembrance, rest on the seventh day.

The Deuteronomy version also contains the remembering aspect, but the commandment begins somewhere else: with a call to *observe* the Sabbath. The first words of the Deuteronomy version are these: "Observe the sabbath day and keep it holy, as the Lord your God commanded you" (Deut 5:12, NRSV). Observe. To observe or keep the Sabbath involves making choices about what we will and won't do on this day. To observe the Sabbath is to demonstrate our obedience to the One who created us and redeems us. The way in which the Sabbath is made holy is connected to the way in which we observe it.

In observant Jewish households, after all preparations are made for the Sabbath and just before sundown on Friday night, two candles are lit. Why two candles? Because of the two versions of the Sabbath commandment. One candle signifies remembering the Sabbath and the other signifies observing the Sabbath.

After the two Sabbath candles are lit, the mother (who traditionally lights these candles) waves her hands over them three times in a semicircular motion, bringing the warmth of the candles to herself. This is a symbolic welcoming of the Sabbath Queen, whom we talked about in the previous chapter. Welcome to our home! We rejoice in your presence! Sabbath has arrived.

Creation, redemption, remember, observe. Here we have the foundation of a Sabbath theology.

Group Meditation

1. Read aloud Exod 20:8–11.

2. Reflect silently on these verses for several minutes.

3. What stood out for you in this passage? How might these verses intersect with your life today?

two

SABBATH, WORK, AND REST
Ceasing and Celebrating

Have you ever played misery poker? Here's how the game works:

ALICIA: "I've been slammed coordinating all the people and details for the upcoming special exhibit. I've had to stay at work past nine every night for two weeks. The exhibit opens next week, which should feel like a relief, but I'm already behind organizing next month's spring gala."

CORY: "Yeah, lots of late nights at work for me, too. And weekends—with this big case getting ready to go to trial, I don't remember the last free weekend I had. I'm running on Red Bull. It makes it hard to plan a family vacation for this summer because I'm expected to be able to rush back to the office when there's any little crisis."

LYNNE: "Try being the personal assistant for the whole family. Here's my day so far: get up and start making lunches, make sure no one overslept, breakfast on the table, out the door to drop kids off at two different schools, back home to get a few things organized for Felicia's birthday party this weekend, back to school to chaperone a field trip, stop at Target to pick up snacks for Justin's soccer game tonight, pick kids up from school, get home and get everyone started on homework and piano practice while trying to get supper ready so we can eat early, drop Justin off at soccer, pick Valerie up from play practice for her show that opens this weekend, drop her off at home, then back to watch Justin's soccer game, where now, at 8:00 p.m., I am getting to sit down for the first time today."

And the game continues, with the players trying to subtly make the case that they are busier and more distraught than the others. The key to winning is one-upping all the other players—if you are the most stressed out, work the longest hours, and are the most miserable, you win! But . . . do you really *want* to win that game?

As much as we might bemoan this pace of life and say that we don't want to win that game or even play it, here's a little-recognized fact: being busy is seen as a badge of honor in our culture. The subtext reads like this: if you are busy, it must be because others need the information, services, or care that only you can provide, and the fact that people are depending on you validates your importance. If you are busy, you must be highly productive, and your high level of productivity translates into social approval and financial gain (if you get paid for your work). And so, while on the one hand we may long for a slower pace of life, on the other hand we might actually feel anxiety by *not* being busy.

In the midst of pressures from without and pressures from within to be busy, the idea of Sabbath rest is profoundly appealing . . . for some. For others it feels like just another stress-inducing obligation to compete with all the other items already on their lengthy to-do lists. And for still others it's so far from their current reality that they simply dismiss the idea of Sabbath rest as unimportant or completely impractical—a quaint practice for simpler people living in simpler times, but not reasonable in our fast-paced, always-connected world.

Let's be honest: if you relate in any way to the misery poker game, a move toward Sabbath rest isn't going to be easy. Is it worth it? Is it worth the effort to push things out of this one day onto the other six days? Is it worth the anxiety that can come from rushing around on Friday or Saturday to get everything done in order to rest on Sunday? More fundamentally, is it even possible in today's culture? Can I possibly get everything done if I take a day off each week to rest? These are important questions to ask, *crucial* questions. Before you settle on your answers, let's try to get a sense of what Sabbath rest might feel and look like.

Celebration and Rest

Celebration is at the heart of Sabbath rest. Imagine for a moment the festive mood of a child's birthday party. Now imagine something of that feeling in connection to a weekly Sabbath. The mood and the focus differ from the other days of the week. The cares and worries of life recede into the background. In Sabbath rest we take time out from everyday life to more intently recognize and experience God's overflowing goodness. We give thanks for our families and friends as we spend time together with them. We celebrate the beauty of all that God has created. Sabbath rest opens us up to these themes of celebration.

Resting on Sabbath involves resting emotionally. Regular weekly life often draws down a person's emotional capacity. In Sabbath rest we press pause to experience refreshment and renewal. This does not mean pretending that the hard relational work that might be on the radar isn't really there, but it might mean saying, "Can we come back to that conversation tomorrow?" Or it might mean shifting to a different mode on the parenting front, rest-ing from the usual consultations or interventions needed to help children learn to show respect, act kindly, and make good choices. Yes, such interactions are important. But putting them aside for a day may help develop other dimensions of the parent-child relationship while providing some emotional rest all the way around. Those sorts of interactions can resume the next day as needed, and in all likelihood nothing will be lost, and much may be gained.

> These are a few activities people have said contribute to their Sabbath celebration:
>
> - eating a meal together
> - playing board games with family and friends
> - sitting around talking and laughing
> - spending some time alone
> - watching old home movies
> - worshipping with one's church family
> - going for a walk
> - taking a nap
>
> Notice that none of these are novel or earth-shattering. The goal is not to make it more entertaining or spectacular than all the possible alternatives. The goal is celebration and connec-tion with God, with others, and with yourself. What helps you celebrate without wearing you out?

We see the element of emotional rest in the Jewish tradition's call to rest even from worry on the Sabbath. Easier said than done, of course! We can't just flip an emotional switch to stop worrying. But we can, by the grace of God, over time train ourselves in this area. When the Worries threaten Sabbath rest, we can hold them up prayerfully in the light of Christ and lay them down at his feet. We can remind ourselves that for this period of time we don't want to dwell on the Worries—we don't need to turn them over and over in our minds right now and we don't need to solve them right now. At the same time, we can choose to refocus on the celebratory aspects of Sabbath and those elements of the day that feel most life-giving. The Worries may come rushing back at once, or they may try to sneak up on us later, and then once again we have the opportunity to bring them out into the open and to present them to God, knowing that God can handle them just fine for us. This is the stuff of spiritual formation; over time, what we practice forms us. Over time, with regular practice we can indeed grow in the ability to set aside the Worries—as well as other emotional struggles—and to thus enter more fully into Sabbath rest.

Another aspect of Sabbath rest is resting intellectually. This involves using our minds differently. The mind that is used all week to plan, problem-solve, design, strategize, gather data, and organize is released from these demands on the Sabbath. Intellectual rest allows us to regain perspective on how our intellectual strivings fit within the broader scope of God's calling on our lives. Sabbath rest invites the development of humility to go along with intellectual prowess. It's not that we try to shut off our brains completely; rather, it's that we use them differently (taking extra time to study Scripture, for example, is a use of our intellect that

> *Reflecting on the Sabbath Experiment:*
> **Family, Fun, and Rest**
>
> "*Once dinner was complete and the table was cleared, we decided to play some board games as a family. The night started off a little rough. We played Little Pet Shop, and the girls argued the whole time. We played Trouble, and the oldest had a really bad attitude. However, by the time we started playing the third game, Apples to Apples, everyone was having fun and laughing. After the games, it was time to put the girls to bed. We all went to bed early, and I woke up Sunday morning feeling more rested than I have for a while.*"
>
> *Andrew*
> *Regional Logistics Manager*

16

has a long history in connection to Sabbath observance). Instead of constantly trying to set speed records on the intellectual race track, for one day a week we take our foot off the gas pedal and allow our minds to move at the pace of a leisurely drive through the countryside. We connect our minds to the rest of Sabbath.

And of course, Sabbath rest involves resting physically. This is the aspect that usually comes to mind first when people think of Sabbath rest, and it's a wonderful dimension of the day. Physical rest is the most obvious type of rest the Israelites experienced when they were delivered from Pharaoh's slave labor camps and given the Sabbath commandment. Whether it is the strain of manual labor, the strain of long hours in the office, or the strain of chores at home, work makes physical demands. Elite athletes know the importance of recovery time after physical exertion. Rest is required for them to be at their peak performance level. Most of us aren't trying to be elite athletes, but the idea connects to the physical rest of Sabbath: this rest is essential for us to live most fully.

Physical rest includes the freedom to get a good night's sleep or to take a refreshing nap. I often hear from those who try the Sabbath

> **Sabbath with Kids?**
>
> A parent came up to me after I taught on Sabbath in an adult Sunday school class. "How do you do this if you have kids?" she asked. "You can't just take the day off from parenting and ignore them." Being a parent of younger children does bring up challenges in relation to Sabbath keeping. While the realities of being a parent may preclude the type of rest we hope for, it does not preclude many of the other elements of Sabbath suggested here. Parents can be sure that children have parts in the Sabbath liturgy used to welcome the day (see Appendix 3). Children might be consulted for ideas for a Sabbath game night or a Sunday afternoon family outing. Being responsible for children may mean that you have to adjust your expectations for the day, but it's not an all-or-nothing proposition—engage the other Sabbath aspects that seem feasible for you and your kids.

Experiment about how refreshed they feel by a good night's sleep. They go to bed relaxed from the slower-paced evening that begins the Sabbath Experiment and then find that they sleep more soundly knowing that they will awake in the morning to a day free from the demands of work.

We live in a culture where being sleep-deprived is often viewed with admiration. It is taken as a sign of commitment and determination. The sports section tells us reverentially about NFL coaches who put in eighteen to twenty-hour days, often sleeping in their offices. I talked with a parent whose two high schoolers had homework loads that required them to stay up past midnight every night. Their sleep deprivation was subtle evidence of the high quality of their private high school education, which would presumably translate into admission at prestigious universities. In the last decade, the sales of energy drinks like Red Bull, Monster, and Rockstar have increased 5000 percent.[1] For many people, the answer to feeling tired is to take a stimulant. Though experts recommend that adults get seven to nine hours of sleep a night, a Gallup poll showed that 40 percent of Americans get less than that.[2]

It turns out that the results go far beyond a person just being a little bit sleepy the next day. Studies show that during our sleeping hours the brain consolidates memory, and the cleaning functions of the brain kick into high gear to clear away toxins and other "brain trash." These renewing brain activities aren't carried out fully when we don't get enough sleep. Studies also show that not getting enough sleep correlates to a whole list of health

> *Reflecting on the Sabbath Experiment:*
> **Four Kids and a Miracle**
>
> *"As part of our Sabbath Experiment, we had a family picnic in the park and sat together on a blanket and ate sandwiches and joked together. After the picnic God graced us with a true miracle. We came home from the park and sat down on the couch, reached for the remote to put a movie on, and remembered we committed to no TV. So we just sat on the couch and talked for 15 minutes or so and here is where the miracle came in: as we talked, our six-year-old feel asleep, quickly followed by our four-year-old falling asleep. Both the babies had already gone down for a nap and for the first time in at least a couple of years, all four kids took a nap. My wife and I stood up and did a happy dance! After a moment of celebration my wife said, 'Hey let's get the dishes done,' and I said, 'Hey let's take a nap!' And we did! We rested for a good hour. It was AMAZING!"*
>
> *Mike*
> *Executive Pastor*

---

1. Ferdman, "Crushing It."
2. Jones, "In U.S., 40 Percent Get Less."

problems including higher rates of anxiety, depression, diabetes, obesity, high blood pressure, cardiovascular disease, asthma, arthritis, and stroke.[3] Some medical experts claim that sleep is on the same level as diet and exercise in contributing to overall health. Though we ourselves are not the primary focal point of Sabbath (*God* is), numerous scientific studies correlate with this theological conviction regarding Sabbath: rest is good for us. Ironically, Sabbath rest takes effort. It takes effort to get out of bed and get to church to worship with your community. It takes effort to teach Sunday school or sing on the worship team. It takes effort to attend to children or to have friends over for a meal. It takes effort to hold to whatever Sabbath disciplines you might choose to embrace. Sabbath rest is not identical with doing nothing. And yet as we plan and prepare in advance as much as possible for Sabbath, the overall tone of the day remains markedly different.

Emotional rest, intellectual rest, and physical rest—these are all aspects of the Sabbath celebration that help us to re-orient ourselves toward our God. Given how common the view is in our culture that lack of rest is normal or even commendable, anyone who is going to try to embrace a

> "We sanctify the Sabbath not only with words and gestures but by the very manner of our repose. The way in which we rest determines whether or not the Sabbath possesses holiness."
> Samuel Dresner, *The Sabbath*[4]

Sabbath way of living may be trying to paddle upstream in a flood-swollen river. In order to say yes to Sabbath rest, we will need to attend to the first part of the commandment: on the Sabbath thou shalt not work. So we turn now to the topic of work.

Work

We can't simply add Sabbath rest on top of everything else. It needs its own space in time. The stoppage of work is what creates this time for Sabbath rest. The stoppage of work doesn't *guarantee* Sabbath rest, but without ceasing from work, Sabbath rest cannot happen.

At the outset, we must note that the Sabbath commandment does not denigrate work. In fact, before calling for work to stop on the Sabbath, the commandment identifies a period of time specifically *for* work: "Six days

---

3. Croft et al., "Association between Perceived," 1–8.

4. Ibid., 29.

you may work and do all your tasks" (Exod 20:9). Work is viewed biblically as something much more than a regrettable necessity. The creation account at the very beginning of the Bible tells us that *God* worked. All the work of creation was seen by God as good. We're told that "on the sixth day God completed all the work that he had done, and on the seventh day God rested from all the work that he had done" (Gen 2:2). In imitation of God, we, too, have work to do.

While work is good, it is only good within limits. We live in a fallen world where some forms of work are oppressive, a drudgery, dehumanizing, or immoral. This work falls outside of God's intended parameters. Workaholism also pushes beyond the parameters of what is good. While, work is part of God's economy—part of God's way of structuring and providing for our families, our communities, and our world, work without limits becomes a cruel taskmaster or a god demanding worship.

> "Is it possible for a human being to do all his [or her] work in six days? Does not our work always remain incomplete?"
> Abraham Joshua Heschel
> *The Sabbath*[5]

If we want to cease working for one day a week, an immediate question arises: what counts as work? The question has been vigorously and extensively debated for millennia—all the way back to the days when the Sabbath command was first given. Why? Because people have wanted to live faithfully. They have wanted to embrace and obey the command to cease work in order to keep the day holy. This requires knowing what work *is*.

In the Jewish tradition, rabbis developed extensive lists and commentaries regarding what counts as work. Drawing on the few explicit instructions in the Hebrew Bible regarding what not to do on the Sabbath and inferences from other passages, the rabbis came up with thirty-nine categories of activities that constitute work. The list includes things like kneading, baking, slaughtering animals, hammering, dyeing wool, weaving, tying a knot, plowing, planting seeds, harvesting, lighting a fire, and extinguishing a fire.[6]

---

5. Heschel, *Sabbath*, 32.

6. Mishnah: Tractate Shabbat, chapter 7 #2. The Mishnah is a collection of Jewish laws and opinions on those laws. These teachings, originally orally transmitted, were written down in the second century CE. The second section, Tractate Shabbat, contains extensive details and discussions regarding Sabbath observance.

In order to be sure that people didn't engage in any of these activities accidentally, the rabbis developed further policies about the policies. Other activities eventually ruled out include cutting your fingernails, writing two or more letters of the alphabet, boiling an egg, and extinguishing a lamp (an exception is made if you are afraid of government officials or robbers coming to your house).[7] And you shouldn't sit down for a hair cut within half an hour of the afternoon prayers that lead up to Sabbath because if the barber's scissors break, they must not be repaired until after the Sabbath (that would constitute work), so you'd only get half a haircut.[8] Work also came to include changing the world in any way by altering or making things, traveling beyond one's community, making plans during the Sabbath for after the Sabbath, and engaging in any activity that constitutes drudgery.[9]

While to us these detailed regulations may seem amusing or stifling in turn, the point of the regulations is this: to honor God by remembering and obeying—remembering that God rested on the seventh day, remembering that God saved the Israelites out of slavery, and obeying God's command to observe Sabbath. To remember and to obey are part of what it means to keep the Sabbath holy.

I'm not suggesting that Christians today should live out these detailed Jewish rules regarding work. If you desire, though, to leave behind work as part of your Sabbath observance, you'll need to ponder what constitutes work in your life.

Some things are obviously work, like the jobs for which we get paid. But work goes beyond that. Stay-at-home parents, for example, don't get paid, but they often work really hard organizing, shuttling, cleaning, cooking, and coordinating to keep a household going. People often ask about these other activities:

- Is gardening work? It involves manual labor, but it is relaxing and life-giving for me. Is it ok or not?

- Is creating art count as work? The tradition has taught that God's creative activity on the first six days constituted God's work, and so when we create we are working, too. But what if creating art leads me into a celebration of beauty, which connects me more deeply with our Creator God?

---

7. Mishnah: Tractate Shabbat, chapter 2 #6.

8. Mishnah: Tractate Shabbat, chapter 1 #2.

9. Dresner, *Sabbath*, 81.

- Is loading the dishwasher work? It seems like one of those household chores that one might want to push out of the Sabbath day, but loading the dishes after a Sabbath meal may help to create a clean, uncluttered environment that is more conducive to rest and relaxation. So, can we do the dishes?

The list could be easily lengthened. Are these things ok or not ok? I would suggest that the answer is a definite "maybe." Let me explain.

Perhaps the reason you're asking these questions is more important than the answers you decide upon. If you are asking because you long for the fullest Sabbath experience possible, because you have a deep desire to taste the Kingdom, and because you desire to rejoice in Sabbath rest before God, perhaps the blessing of the day will be yours regardless of how you answer these questions. On the other hand, if you are asking as a way of looking for a loophole, to find an excuse to not modify anything in your life, or because you don't want to be inconvenienced, the spirit of the day may be missing, and in that case, again, the way you answer these questions might not really matter.

Asking questions about what constitutes work provides both opportunity and danger. The opportunity is to move from talking about the wonderful theological dimensions and interesting historical development of Sabbath to the practical level of making choices

> *Reflecting on the Sabbath Experiment:*
> **Celebrating with Friends**
>
> *"I really enjoyed doing the Sabbath Experiment with my group of girlfriends. We gathered together and had a beautiful dinner to start the Sabbath. I realized that I desire to have more fellowship with the women around me. I can get so purpose oriented and focus only on the 'work' of the ministry that I suppress the personality on the inside of me that will propel me into deeper and meaningful relationships with those who I am called to connect with. There were so many laughs that evening, and as we shared in struggles and testimonies, we strengthened our relationship with one another. During the experiment I felt guilty that I often get so work oriented that I do not always take enough time to worship God and who and what God has placed in my life. I began to lose track of time and before I knew it we were up until almost midnight. The night was a celebration of God and the women around me."*
>
> *Whitley*
> *Seminary Student,*
> *Church Volunteer Coordinator*

about what we will and won't do on this day in our current cultural context. But the danger is that we'll get bogged down in the minutia of these questions and end up like the Pharisees who meticulously tithed even the herbs from their kitchen gardens but neglected the really important aspects of the law: justice, mercy, and faith (Matt 23:23).

Other important questions remain. What about employees who are scheduled to work on Sundays? My mother was a nurse who sometimes had to work Sunday shifts—hospitals can't very well just stop caring for patients one day a week. While employees can make requests, often they have to take whatever shifts they are assigned. Some who get scheduled to work on Sundays choose to have a floating Sabbath that moves to a different day off in the week.

This assumes, of course, that a person *has* a day off in the week. Some people are working seven days a week holding down two or three different jobs just to make rent and put food on the table. To take a day off, even if the schedulers allowed it, would mean coming up short for the basic necessities of life. In these situations, those of us who can choose to Sabbath one day a week have the responsibility to find ways to make this choice possible for others, too. On the personal level, maybe we offer to take our friends' kids for an evening or a weekend so that the parents can have at least a pocket of rest, if not a whole day. Maybe we take over a meal now and then or show up to help tackle a house project. On a macro level, we might consider the idea that we are called to create a society in which *everyone*, even those at the bottom of the pay scale, is paid enough for their jobs so that they can truly afford to rest for at least one day a week. The Sabbath vision is that *everyone* will be able to rest one day a week, not just those at the top of the food chain.

Sabbath must never be used to induce guilt in those who end up working on Sundays (or in anyone, for that matter). As we challenge ourselves in relation to Sabbath observance, we must do so in ways that correlate to the spirit of the day. The Apostle Paul writes, "So don't let anyone judge you about eating or drinking or about a festival, a new moon observance, or sabbaths" (Col 2:16). To use Sabbath as a measuring stick or litmus test of faith and devotion is to misuse Sabbath.

The Pulitzer prize winning author Herman Wouk once reflected on his work producing plays on Broadway. In the midst of that hectic environment, Wouk, an observant Jew, still chose to keep the Sabbath each week. Here's how he recounted that experience:

The Sabbath has cut most sharply athwart my own life when one of my plays has been in rehearsal or in tryout. The crisis atmosphere of an attempt at Broadway is a legend of our time, and a true one; I have felt under less pressure going into battle at sea [he was a World War II Navy veteran]. Friday afternoon, during these rehearsals, inevitably seems to come when the project is tottering on the edge of ruin. I have sometimes felt guilty of treason, holding to the Sabbath in such a desperate situation. But then, experience has taught me that a theatre enterprise almost always is in such a case. Sometimes it does totter to ruin, and sometimes it totters to great prosperity, but tottering is its normal gait, and cries of anguish are its normal tone of voice. So I have reluctantly taken leave of my colleagues on Friday afternoon, and rejoined them on Saturday night. The play has never yet collapsed in the meantime. When I return I find it tottering as before, and the anguished cries as normally despairing as ever. My plays have encountered in the end both success and failure, but I cannot honestly ascribe either result to my observing the Sabbath.[10]

Wouk recognized that the atmosphere of his job would *always* be one of urgency and panic. He recognized that no matter how hard he worked, the

What About Sabbath for Pastors?

Aren't pastors *required* to work on Sundays? Isn't preaching part of a pastor's *work*? Many pastors have navigated this issue by choosing to observe Sabbath on another day of the week. Though the day then loses some of its communal dimension (others aren't observing Sabbath at the same time), this has proven to be a good option of many.

One pastor I know begins his Sabbath at mid-day on Sundays, after the morning worship service has ended, and continues it through mid-day on Monday. This is another option for pastors to consider.

A third option chosen by some pastors is to re-frame what they do on Sundays as worship. For some, writing a sermon is work, and this work is completed before Sunday. They then choose to consider the delivery of the sermon as an act of worship, and conversations with parishioners on Sundays are also framed as worshipful acts. Some who have chosen this approach find that they are helped by moving committee meetings off of Sundays and onto other days of the week, even though this may be less convenient.

One pastor I know makes this the first question he asks his staff at their weekly meeting: "Have you had your Sabbath time this week?" This strongly communicates to the staff what is truly valued in that church. He understands this as a grounding for long-term flourishing in ministry.

---

10. Herman Wouk cited in ibid., 49–50.

sense of crisis would never let up and the desperate frenzy of activity would continue. This perpetual-crisis mode is an experience common to many in our society today. Perhaps you have the experience in your own work of constantly "tottering on the edge of ruin," of always facing crisis and urgency. Wouk made no claim that observing Sabbath made everything turn out rosy. Regardless, he chose to step away from work for one day each week to celebrate Sabbath with his family and his community. Sabbath puts limits on our work so that we might enter into the rest and celebration of God.

I have not offered here a tight definition of what work is, and that's been intentional. My hope is that you will discern with your community what you will consider to be work and how you want work to relate to Sabbath celebration in your life together. Keep in mind that ceasing work is not the ultimate goal of Sabbath. Rather, it is a means of moving toward the Sabbath rest and Sabbath celebration that God desires for us.

Imagine again the festive mood of a child's birthday party. The festive mood of an annual birthday party is made possible on a weekly basis in Sabbath when we make choices to cease from our work for this one day each week. And the festive mood of Sabbath comes to us when we embrace the gifts of emotional, intellectual, and physical rest. In that rest the delight of Sabbath awaits us!

Discussion Questions

1. Play a round of Misery Poker—try to convince others in your group that you are busier and more stressed out than they are (feel free to improvise or exaggerate!). Who's the winner?

2. What feels like celebration for you? How have you incorporated this into Sabbath or how might you?

3. How would you describe your own attitude and experience in relation to Sabbath rest? Does it appeal to you? Does it feel impractical or unimportant? To what extent do you already experience this rest?

4. What counts as work in your life? Discern with your group how you might navigate things you're not sure about counting as work or not.

5. This chapter suggests that there is no one "right" way to observe Sabbath—no exact list of what we should and shouldn't do on that day. Do you find this frustrating or freeing? Would you rather have a clear list of dos and don'ts or do you like this ambiguity? What are the opportunities and dangers in this for you?

⤳ SLOWING DOWN
Sabbath and the Other Nine Commandments

The Sabbath commandment serves as a fascinating link between the first three commandments, which focus on God, and the last six commandments, which focus on relationships within the community. Sabbath contains elements of both sets.

Like the first three commandments, Sabbath draws our attention to God. Up front it is described as "a Sabbath to the Lord your God" (Exod 20:10). In line with the loyalty evoked by the first three commandments, Sabbath observance honors God. The connection goes further.

Is the Sabbath the third or the fourth commandment?

That depends on which of two numbering systems a person uses. While the commandments have always been taken to be ten in number, no numbers are actually assigned to them in scripture. Two numbering systems developed. In this book, I refer to the Sabbath commandment as the fourth commandment, following the numbering tradition held by most Protestant churches and the Eastern Orthodox church. Another numbering system with a long history, used by most Catholics and Lutherans, puts the Sabbath commandment at number three. The difference lies in how the instructions regarding idols and coveting are grouped:

Numbering System A	Numbering System B
1. Have no other gods	1. Have no other gods (and don't make idols of them)
2. Do not make idols	
3. Do not use the Lord's name in vain	2. Do not use the Lord's name in vain
4. Remember the Sabbath	3. Remember the Sabbath
5. Honor father and mother	4. Honor father and mother
6. Do not kill	5. Do not kill
7. Do not commit adultery	6. Do not commit adultery
8. Do not steal	7. Do not steal
9. Do not testify falsely	8. Do not testify falsely
10. Do not covet	9. Do not covet neighbor's house
	10. Do not covet neighbor's wife, servants, livestock, or anything else

Though different numbering systems exist, the content remains the same.

The first commandment is set up by a reference to the exodus event: "I am the Lord your God who brought you out of Egypt, out of the house of slavery" (Exod 20:2). The old context is named as a way of juxtaposing their previous life with what life is to be like in the new social system set forth by the God of Israel. Then the first commandment is given: "You must have no other gods before me" (v. 3). Leave behind the enslaving social system of Egypt. And with it, leave behind the gods that underwrite that system of endless production for the benefit of Pharaoh and the other elites.

The connection to Egypt that sets up the first commandment is found one other place in the Ten Commandments: within the Sabbath commandment as found in Deuteronomy: "Remember that you were a slave in Egypt" (5:15). By remembering on the Sabbath that they were slaves in Egypt, the Israelites would all the more celebrate living under the God who delivered them into the freedom of a new social arrangement. The fourth commandment connects to the first because Sabbath observance is an affirmation that they have left behind the enslaving gods of Egypt and have no other gods before Yahweh. As Walter Brueggemann puts it, "Sabbath becomes a decisive, concrete, visible way of opting for and aligning with the God of rest" rather than with Pharaoh's gods.[1]

Sabbath has connections to the last six commandments as well. The Sabbath commandment is concerned for relationships within the community, as are the commandments that follow. The Sabbath commandment carefully names how people in the community are to relate to each other when it comes to Sabbath rest: *everyone* in the community—family, servants, foreigners—is to be granted rest. This means that relationships structured by privilege or position are put into a new frame by the Sabbath. By extending rest to everyone, Sabbath overcomes the social classifications that otherwise shape relationships.

The concern for relationships within the community reaches something of a climax in the tenth commandment about not coveting.[2] This commandment can be understood in one sense to be a sweeping statement that includes within it the more specific commandments leading up to it. Commandments five through nine can all be understood as putting in check actions that serve our covetous impulses, impulses named in the tenth commandment. The desire for other people's things that is specifically called out in the culminating tenth commandment is also put in check

---

1. Brueggemann, *Sabbath as Resistance,* 10.

2. Ibid., 69.

by the Sabbath commandment. On the Sabbath, we stop working, which means that we stand in defiant resistance to the covetous forces that would drive us to work without ceasing.

In continuity with the first three commandments, Sabbath has a focus on the God who delivers out of slavery. And like the last six commandments, Sabbath is concerned about peaceable relationships within the whole community. In its bridging role, the Sabbath commandment connects love of God and love of people.

Group Meditation

1. Read aloud Deut 5:6–21.

2. Reflect silently on these verses for several minutes.

3. What stood out for you in this passage? How might these verses intersect with your life today?

three

SABBATH AND TECHNOLOGY
Connecting in a Disconnected World

Living in a connected age opens up a whole new world of possibilities. Through Facebook, we can know a bit about what's going on in the lives of dozens of our friends around the world in a way that was simply not possible a generation ago. A text message lets us know that our daughter is running late but will be there soon. When a military conflict erupts in another part of the world, the internet allows us instantly to click on news stories that tell us what's happening on the ground at that moment. The technology of email allows us to send a note, receive concert tickets electronically, or instantly send out a conference schedule.

I remember my first foray onto the internet in the early 1990s. I took a class at a community college about how to connect from home to the internet using a dial-up connection and how to go to web pages. Search engines were an obscure and rudimentary concept at the time; being unaware of them, I had to know the address of a site I wanted to visit or find it from a list of sites on a handout. The web pages I remember accessing were mainly lists of things like others' favorite books or songs, all appearing as white text on a black background—no pictures or videos at that point. It never crossed my mind to pause and consider how I might be shaped relationally and morally by using this technology. But now, twenty-plus years later, I find those questions unavoidable—at least if I am going to accept responsibility for my own spiritual formation in this digital age. Sabbath keeping helps to raise and answer questions about spiritual formation in an age of digital connectedness. It clarifies a set of choices we have about how we are going to live in this chapter of history.

Most people have a sense that allowing technology to be all-pervasive in our lives isn't a good thing. Don't panic! I'm not setting you up for an all-out assault on the role of digital technology in our lives. I am not going to urge you to go back in time to some pre-technological golden age. I am not going to suggest that texting is of the devil or that the problems of humanity would all be resolved if everyone canceled their Facebook accounts. I don't think that Sabbath living requires us to eliminate these technologies from our lives. But in a time when few people seem to be making specific choices to put any limits on texting, social media, or other uses of digital technology, Sabbath may in fact call for some limits if we are to experience Sabbath's deepest blessings—not only on the Sabbath, but on the other six days, too.

Our lives are full of technology, ranging from cars to indoor plumbing to clocks to electrical outlets. I'm focusing here on digital technology, or what Nicholas Carr calls intellectual technologies—"tools we use to extend or support our mental powers."[1] Included are technologies such as the internet and texting—all the ways we gather information, communicate with one another, and interact with the world through digital media. These technologies occupy our time differently than other technologies and are much more influential in shaping our patterns of thinking, relationships, and habits. This narrower category is what I have in mind when I talk about technology in this section.

If a Sabbath practice of disconnecting for twenty-four hours seems like an easy one for you, go ahead and skip this chapter. But if you find yourself resisting or revolting against it, or if it just seems impossible, I invite you to live in that tension for the next few pages. Chew on why a person might choose to live in this way. Contemplate the ways digital technology, Sabbath keeping, and our relationships with God and with each other might intersect. Then decide how your choices to use or not use digital technology might help you live the sort of connected life God desires for us.

> As we look at the role of technology in our lives, imagine what it might be like for one full day to:
>
> - turn off your cell phone and put it in a drawer (or have a friend hide it!).
> - keep your computer and tablet turned off—not surfing the web, not checking email, not keeping up on Facebook.
> - engage in activities and relationships that invite you to be present, undistracted, and deeply connected to God, others, and creation.

---

1. Carr, *Shallows*, 44.

The Connected Mind

Do you remember learning somewhere along the line that after early child-hood you have all the brain cells you'll have for the rest of your life? For decades this was the dominant scientific view. It held that other types of cells could reproduce (you could grow new skin cells or new muscle cells), but your brain cells could not increase in number or grow. This view has been obliterated by new research on the brain over the last twenty years.

As it turns out the wiring in our brains is not permanently fixed at some young age after all. Study after study has shown that our brains can actually change over the course of an entire lifetime, a dynamic called neuroplasticity. These changes can include both the number of neurons (brain cells) we have as well as the ways in which these neurons are bundled together.

In one study on neuroplasticity, a team of German neuroscientists examined the brains of medical students before and after an intense period of studying.[2] German medical students have to take a comprehensive exam after two years of classroom work. The exam involves both written and oral components covering biology, chemistry, biochemistry, physics, human anatomy, and physiology. Preparation for the exam involves three months of intense daily study sessions. The researchers took magnetic resonance images (MRIs) of the students' brains at the start of the three month study period and again at the time of the comprehensive exam.

MRIs conducted at the time of the comprehensive exam—after the medical students had been studying intensely for three months—showed that significant changes had occurred in their brains since the scans done three months earlier: the hippocampus of participants' brains increased in size. This corroborates other research showing that the brain itself actually changes physically in response to the ways it is used.

The ability of the brain to adapt and produce new growth has also been shown in studies of people who have had strokes. A stroke victim commonly leaves the hospital with diminished motor skills in a hand or arm, but in the weeks and months that follow, those motor skills often im-prove. How does that happen? Neuroscientists have shown that it happens because of adaptations that take place in the patient's brain. To compensate for the stroke-damaged part of the brain, other parts of the brain change to take over various functions. One of the most common adaptations is the

---

2. Draganski et al., "Temporal and Spatial."

re-bundling of some neurons used to control the face to take over for damaged neurons that had been used to control the hand.[3] Stroke victims commonly regain some of their lost hand dexterity as a result of these changes in the brain.

Neuroplasticity works in another way, too. The parts of our brains that are not used very much can shrink. Think of a broken arm in a cast—the unused arm muscles atrophy from not being exercised during the healing time. The same thing basically happens to our brains.

This has been shown in experiments on people who have gone blind. When a person's eyes stop working, the part of the brain used for sight shrinks. At the same time, while the unused part of the brain becomes smaller, the part used for hearing, which now experiences extra demand, increases in size. Neurons that were used for seeing are re-bundled with the parts of the brain used for hearing.[4] The structure of the brain changes.

Our brains are also re-wired by the ways in which we use the internet. In one study, the brain activity of experienced web users was compared to that of novice web users.[5] Brain scans showed that when doing Google searches, the experienced web users had extensive front left brain activity while the novice web users had little or no activity in this region of the brain. For the next five days, the novice web users spent at least an hour a day online doing Google searches.

On the sixth day, their brains were scanned again while they were using the internet. Remarkably, the front left brains of the novice web users now showed the same widespread activity as seen in this region of the experienced web users' brains. The physical patterns in the brain had been changed dramatically in just five days.

Texting, checking Facebook, and scrolling through Twitter give our brains repeated practice in:

- scanning massive amounts of information (when I'm doing research through a database, I will commonly scan through a hundred or more search results),

- distinguishing between what is most important and what is peripheral (I've developed a pretty good ability to ignore sidebar ads),

---

3. Cramer, "Repairing the Human Brain," 277.

4. Carr, *Shallows*, 29.

5. Small et al., "Your Brain on Google," cited in Carr, 121.

- analyzing the content (will this page help me set up my wireless home printer network or do I need to click on something else?),

- and making quick decisions (read or click to the next page?).

The neurons and synapses used for this type of thinking grow bigger, and as a result, this sort of thinking becomes easier. Then, because our brains like to do what they are strong at, they crave more of this type of use. The activities we choose and the mapping of our brains are part of a mutually reinforcing cycle.

The ways in which we use our brains in relation to internet usage can have numerous benefits. People can experience the strengthening of those parts of their brains used for fast-paced problem solving, and they can experience a slight expansion of their brains' working memory capacity. Studies also show that internet usage may help older people to keep their minds sharp. Further, internet usage has been shown to strengthen visual-spatial skills.[6]

The use of digital technology to surf the internet or text a friend has other effects on our brains, also. Here's a scene you've probably seen in the last day: a guy texts a friend, then checks his Facebook page, then clicks on a page to see last night's baseball scores, then clicks through to a story on a player's injury, then responds to the text on his phone that just arrived. Using our brains in this way covers a lot of ground, but the type of thinking developed is scattered and shallow. Skimming media-rich web pages exposes us to large quantities of information and visuals, but the brain's ability to actually learn is diminished and understanding is weakened.[7] We become less able to engage in undistracted, deep thinking.

> *Reflecting on the Sabbath Experiment:*
>
> **No Electronics**
>
> *"For longer term embracing, the idea of no electronics on the Sabbath resonated with me because at work that is what I do; I use electronics because I have to, especially being in the IT profession. I think that with the world becoming more electronic, we neglect the beauty that nature has to offer."*
>
> *Bruce*
> *Technology Support*
> *Professional*

6. Carr, *Shallows*, 122, 139, 141.

7. Ibid., 129.

A study conducted by Ziming Liu, a professor at San José State University, showed that because of the internet people are spending more time reading, but the type of reading being done "is characterized by browsing and scanning, keyword spotting, one-time reading, [and] non-linear reading . . . while less time is spent on in-depth reading and concentrated reading."[8] Thus the neurons and synapses used for this latter type of reading are being exercised less. As a result, it becomes physiologically more difficult to follow an extended line of thinking regarding poverty reduction, to take in a nuanced description of a political conflict, or to meditate on the words and ways of God. It's like trying to run a 10k race when you've mainly been using your legs to walk from the couch to the refrigerator. You may be able to cover the distance, but you'd find it much easier if you had been using your legs to run daily for months.

The ways you use your brain are connected to how you express your love of God. Jesus quotes the ancient Hebrew *shema* when he answers a scribe's question about which commandment is the greatest: " . . . you must love the Lord your God with all your heart, with all your being, *with all your mind*, and with all your strength (Mark 12:30, my italics; cf. Deut 6:4). These phrases are different ways of saying the same thing: love God with every fiber of your being, with the fullness of who you are as a person. Our minds are included in this fullness, so our minds are part of what we use to love God with holistic devotion.

The shape of this devotion is illuminated by the psalmist who writes poetically that the righteous "love the Lord's Instruction, and they recite God's Instruction day and night!" (Ps 1:2). Extending this idea, the Christian tradition shows us that the path of faithfulness and spiritual growth includes times of sustained prayer, times of silence and stillness, and times of contemplating who God is and the type of life God calls us to live. These activities require us to use the parts of our brains that allow us to think calmly, to be undistracted, and to focus for extended periods of time.

You can see the problem. The use of digital technology does not foster the type of thinking that develops the brain circuits needed for contemplation, undistracted prayer, and other such dimensions of spiritual formation. As Carr points out, "It's possible to think deeply while surfing the Net . . . but that's not the type of thinking the technology encourages and

---

8. Liu, "Reading Behavior," 705.

rewards."[9] It *is* the type of thinking encouraged and rewarded by disconnecting, slowing down, and embracing Sabbath.

Rabbi Abraham Joshua Heschel made an observation over fifty years ago that is still relevant today. He wrote, "The solution to [human]kind's most vexing problems will not be found in renouncing technical civilization, but in attaining some degree of independence from it."[10] Along these lines, I'm not suggesting here that we should never use the internet or cut out texting completely. I *am* suggesting, however, that we need to set these technologies aside at times if we are to develop our brains for certain dimensions of spiritual formation. A Sabbath rhythm of life invites us into at least a day each week when we think in ways that use these different parts of our brains.

Compassion and the Internet

Sabbath, digital technology, and spiritual formation have another point of intersection: compassion. Embedded in the Sabbath commandment is a call to compassion. Recall the scope of the command: Sabbath rest is to extend to one's sons and daughters, male and female slaves, livestock, and foreigners who are present. Pharaoh's brutality is not replicated but replaced with a way of treating others that mirrors the compassion of the One True God. Each week, Sabbath reminds us to be compassionate toward others.

How compassionate are you? As compassionate as you would like to be? More compassionate than you used to be? In writing to the church in Colossae, the Apostle Paul instructs the faithful to clothe themselves with compassion, kindness, humility, gentleness, and patience (Col 3:12). Paul assumes that we can change or increase our capacity for compassion. Twenty-first century brain research supports Paul's assumption.

In a study conducted at the University of Wisconsin-Madison, Helen Weng and her colleagues sought to find out if people could increase their levels of compassion through training, and if brain changes brought about by the training could be correlated to increased compassion.[11] At the start of the experiment, all participants were given MRI scans. Then one group was given compassion training for two weeks, which involved spending half an hour a day in compassion meditation following online audio in-

---

9. Carr, *Shallows*, 116.

10. Heschel, *Sabbath*, 28.

11. Weng et al., "Compassion Training."

structions. A second group was given a type of training that focused on reducing their negative emotions in response to a stressful event.

At the end of the two-week period, participants again underwent MRI scans, this time while viewing images of suffering. The brains of those who underwent compassion training showed increased levels of neural activity in the inferior parietal cortex and the dorsalateral prefrontal cortex, parts of the brain associated with empathy and emotion regulation. The changes in neural activity showed that compassion training resulted in *physical changes to the brain*. Then the researchers went on to a second part of the experiment.

Each research subject played a redistribution game online with two anonymous players, one who was the dictator and the other who was the victim. While the research subject observed, the dictator, who had been given 10 dollars, gave 1 dollar to the victim, who had no money. The scenario was set up to communicate that this small amount of money transfer was unfair. The research subject, who had 5 dollars, could then choose to give any portion of that 5 dollars to the victim, knowing that the dictator would then be required to give twice that amount to the victim. The research subjects also knew that they could keep any part of the 5 dollars not given to the victim. Would the compassionate expression of generosity be different between the two original groups of research subjects? It was.

Those whose MRI scans had shown increased activity in the inferior parietal cortex and the dorsalateral prefrontal cortex gave more of their 5 dollars to the victim. That is to say, those with higher activity in certain parts of their brains acted more compassionately. According to the researchers, "these results suggest that compassion can be cultivated with training and that greater altruistic behavior may emerge from increased engagement of neural systems implicated in understanding the suffering of other people, executive and emotional control, and reward processing."[12] To put it another way, the researchers concluded that something of a virtuous cycle exists: compassion training can change our brains, and as a result of these brain changes, we are more likely to act compassionately. The research corroborates the Apostle Paul's view from two thousand years ago that we can grow in our compassion!

Brain research has revealed something else related to compassion: our brains are slow to feel it. In a University of Southern California study, Mary Helen Immordino-Yang and her colleagues compared how the brain reacts

12. Ibid., 1171.

when a person witnesses a variety of scenarios designed to elicit compassion. The study showed that brain activity peaks the quickest in response to witnessing physical pain.[13] So for example, neural pathways are activated the quickest when you see a child get hurt on the playground or when you see a YouTube video of a person getting beat up. Brain activity associated with compassion for physical pain peaks at around six seconds after the stimulus.

Compassion for emotional or psychological pain takes longer to register in our brains. When presented with a situation such as a refugee suffering deep emotional pain from the death of a loved one or a person suffering from the loss of a job, brain activity in response peaks at around twelve seconds.

While the response rate to emotional suffering is longer than the response rate to physical suffering, both responses are relatively slow. The brain responds in a fraction of a second when you are frightened by a crashing noise behind you or if you accidentally touch a hot burner. In comparison, the six to twelve seconds it takes for our brains to fully engage the neural pathways related to compassion is a glacial pace.

> *Reflecting on the Sabbath Experiment:*
> ### Disconnecting
>
> *"Another aspect of the Sabbath Experiment that I thoroughly enjoyed was abstaining from any media. I did not use my phone or computer, watch television, or listen to the radio. This allowed me to be aware of how much of a part of my normal life these mediated experiences are.*
>
> *While this was difficult to observe, it kept my focus on those who were around me, and I had a great time spending the Sabbath day with friends. I had time to spend in conversations and play games, but I spent a good deal of my Sabbath day reading as well. It was very refreshing for me to sit back and read on Sunday afternoon, without any nagging thought in my head that I had other things to take care of."*
>
> Chris
> Associate Pastor

Now consider how this relates to the way I check Google news several times a day. I click on the shortcut in my browser, the web page comes up, and I scan down the list of headlines. A quick glance tells me that dozens of people died from a suicide bombing or that multiple families lost their homes to a tornado. Think about how this relates to the brain research on

---

13. Immordino-Yang et al., "Neural Correlates," 8024.

compassion. While I may retain a snippet of factual data about the story, the research shows that I have not given my brain sufficient time to respond with compassion. If I want to set myself up to be more compassionate, I must find ways and times to slow down—for the sake of my brain and for the sake of others. As the lead researcher Immordino-Yang observed, "If things are happening too fast, you may not ever fully experience emotions about other people's psychological states and that would have implications for your morality."[14] That's a problem for me as a Christian. It's a problem to which we must attend.

If we want to become more compassionate people, we need to at least occasionally slow down the ways we process information in this digital age. That might involve reading a lengthy article rather than just a headline, or it might involve creating other space in time for a slower pace of reflection. A space in time such as Sabbath.

We Prepare for Sabbath, Sabbath Prepares Us

Remember that the Sabbath makes a claim on us. To enter Sabbath time, to keep the Sabbath holy, requires preparation. The more obvious sorts of preparation are things like inviting friends to join us for a Sunday meal, or filling up the car with gas and buying groceries on Saturday so that on Sunday we can step out of the system of buying and selling. We might also consider how we prepare our brains for the Sabbath.

In light of the research we've reviewed, one step in preparing our brains for Sabbath observance could be to block out time each day to disconnect from digital technology. You might choose to set aside the first hour or two of your day and not check text messages or email during that time. Maybe it's going for a daily walk without your cell phone on. Perhaps the evening meal becomes a tech-free zone, or maybe it's the hour or two before bedtime (research shows that this also helps people go to sleep more quickly). Studies show that even small amounts of time spent using our brains in specific ways can enlarge and strengthen the correlated parts of our brains. As we set aside digital technology here and there during our week, we open up time for other ways of using our brains.

---

14. From an interview with Mary Helen Immordino-Yang regarding the research project cited above, found in "Twitter and Facebook."

Sabbath preparation is not just subtraction; it's also addition. What might you want to *include* in terms of brain use as Sabbath preparation? Reading a book, space for longer conversations with family and friends, prayer and meditation, crossword or Sudoku puzzles, a hobby, Bible study—what fits best for you? What leads you into calm, attentive thinking? What helps you experience compassion and empathy? Some people have jobs that involve their brains in this type of thinking. Others need supplementary brain work. We are all quite aware of the benefits of physical exercise several times a week. We will benefit also from exercising our brains in these or similar ways several times a week. It's a step in preparing the actual structures of our brains so that we are physiologically better equipped to ponder the depths and mysteries of God on the Sabbath.

This idea of preparation flows not just toward Sabbath but also out of Sabbath. We prepare for the Sabbath, and Sabbath prepares us. By entering into Sabbath time and by making choices that encourage the spirit of Sabbath, we may strengthen certain parts of our brains in ways that allow us to be more focused, think more deeply, and be more compassionate at other times of the week too. Our brain cells and neural pathways are developed through weekly Sabbath observance to see and experience Sabbath moments throughout the other six days of the week also.

Practical Steps for Sabbath Disconnecting

My friend Doug is a pastor who makes Tuesdays his Sabbath. If you email Doug on a Tuesday, you'll get this auto reply: "Today is the day I honor God with Sabbath rest. I will reply to emails tomorrow. Thanks for understanding." Not only does he kindly notify others as to why he's not responding right away, but in doing so he implicitly invites them to think about Sabbath in their own lives and shows that Sabbath keeping is indeed a real option even in today's culture. It can be difficult—even excruciating—at first, but try it: each week for the twenty-four hours of Sabbath, try setting an out-of-office reply for your email saying that you'll get back to them after the Sabbath, and then don't check it.

Texting can be an even bigger challenge, because people expect text message responses even faster than email replies. But if your concern is for others' possible offence at not receiving a quick text back during your Sabbath day, you could set an auto-response on your cell phone like for your email. Or you might just gradually let people in your life know that you won't be responding to texts on the Sabbath. People will likely respect your choice. Such a choice says that you're creating an alternate culture. You haven't rejected technology (you still have your phone!), but you have chosen for one seventh of the week to experience God's world differently.

Given the current culture, the idea of disconnecting for one day a week may seem irresponsible, unnecessary, or even ludicrous. "I need to be reachable. I enjoy being connected, so it's part of my Sabbath rest. Don't get legalistic with me—I can text and surf the net and still keep the spirit of Sabbath." Maybe that works for some people. Others find the idea of disconnecting from cyberspace for a day to be truly appealing. This is seen in the broader culture outside of religious contexts in the form of digital detox retreats, device-free bar nights and tech-free cold spots. An NPR story told of a Massachusetts family that instituted a weekly internet Sabbath for reasons other than religious; from Friday night through Sunday night they set aside video games, computers, and cell phones.[15] If people with no particular religious motives see a good in this, how much more should Christians, who have a Sabbath invitation going back thousands of years, see its good! And in fact,

---

Reflecting on the Sabbath Experiment:

My Cell Phone

"Through the Sabbath Experiment I saw how attached to my phone I am! My constant connectedness is reinforced by family, friends, and coworkers. When I receive a text or email, I typically respond immediately.

I felt a little anxious at first when I put my phone on silent (actually, my husband turned my phone off for me), but as the day wore on, I was so focused on spending time with my family and enjoying the afternoon that I didn't really miss it anymore. Most importantly, this exercise helped me to be present in the moment, with no distractions.

With not being able to check emails or text messages I was able to enjoy Sunday afternoon with my husband. We played a board game (which we never do) and had great conversation. I took a nap, which I also never do. The Sabbath experience helped me rest and delight in God's creation in ways that I haven't done so in awhile."

Maressa
Associate Pastor

---

15. Adler, "How Our Digital Devices."

when I talk to Christian groups and individuals about Sabbath, for many the idea of disconnecting for a day is indeed appealing; it stirs in their hearts a longing for a simpler life, a longing for a slower pace, a longing for rest and laughter and reflection.

So here's the rub: it takes significant effort to limit or eliminate one's use of technology for one day a week, but the path to joy, celebration, and the connections that God wants for us may require it. If you're at all like me, you'd just as soon have the benefits without the exertion required to approach time in this manner, but it doesn't seem to work that way. It's ironic, but entering Sabbath rest requires a lot of effort.

Now let's step back for some perspective. Sabbath observance does not demand any of this in relation to technology. There's no one "right" way to use or not use technology on Sundays. Even if the general direction of this chapter makes sense

Sabbath, Technology, and Children

Once after I gave a talk on Sabbath and technology, a parent came up to me and said, "My kids are already resistant to coming to church with us. I'm afraid that if I make Sundays screen-free that it will only increase their resistance toward church and faith." If you're in a situation like this, perhaps it would be helpful to start somewhere else with Sabbath observance in your family. Start with easier things, like welcoming the Sabbath by making the kids' favorite meal—they're not going to resist that Sabbath practice! You can also model a Sabbath rhythm through your own choices for the day. You might explain to them why you're choosing not to do any work for the day, and about how that opens up time for the whole family to do something fun together—then actually *do* something fun! You might talk about how part of Sabbath is celebrating with the community, and then invite others over for a barbeque. And you might explain why you yourself are choosing to put aside various forms of technology for the day and what that means in connection to your own faith journey. None of these ideas make demands of the kids, but as they watch how you live, the blessings of Sabbath will touch their lives, too.

to you, the options for implementation are many. In my own family, disconnecting from technology on Sundays is not an absolute. Sunday mornings are screen-free times, but in the afternoon when we come home from worshipping with our church family, the kids can turn on the computer or TV. I stay checked out from email until after supper that night, but I might watch a basketball game on TV in the afternoon. The tension is to put in place a clear structure (the Sabbath Queen) without allowing it to become so rigid or oppressive that it obscures the spirit of the day (the Sabbath Bride).

Try it—try a tech-free day each week for a month. That's not long enough to probe the full depths of the practice, but it's a good start. Then ask yourself this question: does disconnecting in these ways enhance or detract from the desires of your heart and the good of your community as you seek to live faithfully?

Discussion Questions:

1. How has technology benefitted and detracted from your relationships?

2. Do you currently have tech-free times in your week? Describe them.

3. What would be the biggest challenges for you in altering your use of technology for the Sabbath?

4. Where do you currently find space in your week for deeper, reflective thinking and being?

⋟ SLOWING DOWN
Sabbath in Exodus 31

I have a framed picture that shows a rainbow over an old red barn. It's from the farm in North Dakota where my grandparents lived when I was growing up. While the picture with the rainbow connects me to a place that is deeply important to me, rainbows carry a meaning that transcends place: God designated them as a global sign of the covenant that God made with Noah to never again send such a flood upon the earth (Gen 9:8–17). Later, in the Sinai wilderness, God makes another covenant with the Israelites (Exod 20–31). With this covenant, God designates another sign to mark it. That marker is Sabbath: "Be sure to keep my sabbaths, because the Sabbath is a sign between me and you in every generation so you will know that I am the LORD who makes you holy" (Exod 31:13, 16b).

Awareness of this day as covenant sign brings a whole new dimension to the meaning of Sabbath! Yes, Sabbath is about rest and refreshment. Yes, Sabbath is about obedience and ceasing work. Yes, Sabbath is about community and joy. But in addition to these other meanings, Sabbath is designated by God as a sign of covenant. No other commandment or law holds this place of honor, and no geographical location or physical structure carries this designation. The role of ongoing sign of the covenant is reserved for the Sabbath.

Sabbath can continue to function as covenantal sign for us today. It can point us to the multiple covenants God has made with us, which climax in the new covenant we have in and through Christ. This new covenant involves forgiveness, love, and newness of life, which are lived out communally as social ethics by the followers of Christ. Just as Sabbath functioned as a way for the Israelites to recommit weekly to the Sinai covenant, Sabbath can serve as a weekly opportunity for us to recommit to the redeeming and restoring covenant God graciously offers to us.

In the Jewish tradition, people speak of "making" Sabbath. The Hebrew word that is most often translated as "make" or "do" (*asah*) is usually translated into English here in Exod 31:16 as "observe." This is a fine translation, but by translating it as "make" we can more easily see the parallel structure and nuance of meaning present in the Hebrew: the Israelites are to *make* Sabbath (v. 16) as a sign that God *made* the heavens and the earth and then rested (v. 17; the root word for "make" in both verses is the same: *asah*). God made creation, we make Sabbath.

This points to a difference between the rainbow and Sabbath as covenant signs. The rainbow appears because God sets it in the clouds. But God does not make the Sabbath appear. The Sabbath appears when people make it. The seventh/first day comes regardless of our actions or observances, but that day does not constitute a Sabbath unless we form it into Sabbath time. It is our making the Sabbath and keeping it holy that makes it function as a perpetual sign of the covenant (v. 16). We have a significant responsibility as co-signers of this covenant!

Holiness is another aspect of Sabbath that is deeply embedded in Exodus 31. Three connections are made here between Sabbath and holiness. First, it is God who makes people holy and Sabbath reminds us of this: "Sabbath is a sign . . . that I am the LORD who makes you holy" (v. 13; "make holy" comes from a different Hebrew word than "make" described above). God's transforming work makes us more and more like the Divine (2 Peter 1:4). It is by the power of the Holy Spirit at work within us that we become the holy people ("saints" in most English translations) that God desires us to be (Eph 3:14–21). Sabbath keeping remains a means by which we can acknowledge God's gracious, transforming initiatives that form us into a holy people.

Exodus 31 then shows a second connection between Sabbath and holiness: "Keep the Sabbath, because it is holy for you" (v. 14). What might this mean that it is holy for *us*? Usually things that are set aside as holy are set aside for *God*, not for people. But here it's different. Perhaps Sabbath itself is holy for us because it blesses us in return for our keeping it. Perhaps Sabbath itself is holy for us because of the way it contributes to making us a holy people.

With the third connection to holiness, we ourselves drop from focus: Sabbath "is holy to the LORD" (v. 15). It is set aside for the Lord in a special way. It is observed in a way that makes it acceptable and pleasing in the sight of God. The ways in which we observe the Sabbath determine the extent to which it is holy to the Lord.

Throughout Scripture, the meaning of Sabbath keeps shifting and expanding. Here in Exodus 31 we see its covenantal dimension highlighted for the first time and its holiness dimension expanded.

Group Meditation

1. Read aloud Exod 31:12–17.

2. Reflect silently on these verses for several minutes.

3. What stood out for you in this passage? How might these verses intersect with your life today?

four

SABBATH ETHICS
With Justice for All

When most people think of Sabbath, they don't think of ethics or social justice. Sabbath is most commonly connected to themes of rest, reflection, and refreshment. These are life-giving themes to be embraced and celebrated, but they don't exhaust the meanings embedded in Sabbath. Honoring the Sabbath also has ethical implications for our lives.

Sabbath is not intended to be a protective cocoon that isolates us from the big bad world out there. On the contrary, as we understand more fully the theological dimensions of Sabbath, we will find ourselves challenged to engage more passionately and lovingly with the broader society rather than isolating ourselves from it. This engagement will not be simply an endorsement of what the dominant culture has to offer. It will be an engagement that affirms what is good in a culture, critiques a culture's practices of injustice and immorality, and seeks to change the way things are to better approximate the Kingdom of God. This is doing Christian ethics. Let's look at some ways in which Sabbath observance might relate to this.

We're People, Not Machines

Sabbath trains us to view one another fundamentally as relational beings who are invited into a covenant with God rather than as machines for production and wealth accumulation. The ethical challenge in this for us is to confront and reject cultural views and practices that treat people mainly in

46

terms of how they contribute to economic gain. It's an ethical issue today, and it was an ethical issue back when the Israelites were slaves in Egypt.

As slaves, the Israelites were viewed by Pharaoh in terms of their productive capacity and therefore their ability to increase Pharaoh's wealth. The Israelites were forced to manufacture bricks (Exod 5) in order that Pharaoh could expand his supply cities (Exod 1:11). The supply cities were where Pharaoh stored his excess grain which he could then sell when the market suited him.

The most profitable time for Pharaoh to sell his surplus grain was when others were desperate for food, and this was the case during drought years. Those in desperate need were willing to spend all their money and sell all their livestock to buy food. When these liquid assets were used up, the people were eventually willing to sell their land and even their own bodies in order to buy food (Gen 47:13–27).

Pharaoh's vast storage facilities allowed him to take advantage of these drought conditions to maximize his wealth accumulation. To build these storage facilities, bricks were required. And to supply the bricks, the Israelites' slave labor was required. The Israelites were just a cog in Pharaoh's money-making machine. He fed his insatiable appetite for accumulation with no regard for the human cost. Since the ways in which we structure our economics reflect our understanding of our gods, the Egyptian gods would have been understood by Pharaoh's regime to be supportive of his oppressive economic policies.[1] The gods of Egypt were complicit in a cultural system that dehumanized a segment of the population.

All this is in view when God gives the Israelites the Ten Commandments. God introduces the first commandment by proclaiming, "I am the LORD your God who brought you out of Egypt, out of the house of slavery. You must have no other gods before me" (Exod 20:2–3). Out of Egypt . . . out of slavery . . . no other gods. These introductory words to the first commandment are a link to the fourth commandment. With this opening statement, as Walter Brueggemann points out, "the Sabbath commandment is drawn into the exodus narrative, for the God who rests is the God who emancipates *from slavery* and consequently *from the work system of Egypt* and *from the gods of Egypt* who require and legitimate that work system."[2] Thus the Ten Commandments begin with God setting up a contrast between God's self and the gods of Egypt. God's alternative culture

---

1. Brueggemann, *Sabbath as Resistance*, 3.

2. Ibid., 2.

will be based on covenant (relationships) rather than commodities (bricks, grain).[3] The God of Israel is laying out a vision of shalom, a way of living that is markedly different from Pharaoh's.

Back in Egypt, the Israelite slaves were given production quotas they had to meet or else they'd be punished. When the Israelites requested time off to celebrate a festival to God (Exod 5:1), Pharaoh went ballistic! He was furious. Not only did he deny their request, but he increased their work load. While they were required to meet the same production quotas, they additionally had to gather the straw for making the bricks, a resource that had previously been provided for them. And if the quotas weren't met, they'd be made to suffer even more. In order to expand the wealth of the top dog, the economic system sought to squeeze more and more productive capacity out of the slaves while providing them with fewer resources. Efficiency was harnessed in a way that increased wealth production while also increasing human suffering. Efficiency is a demanding god.

Don't get me wrong—I value efficiency. When I have several errands to run, I like to plan out the order in which I'll do them so that I spend the least amount of time in the car driving. When I am standing in a checkout line, I hope the clerk at the front of the line works efficiently so that my wait is short. Efficiency can allow us to use our natural resources more wisely, and efficiencies of production and distribution bring down the price of the replacement rice cooker our household is looking to buy right now.

However, efficiency has repeatedly become the taskmaster of oppressive economic systems, a harsh slave driver that brutalizes people.

- For the sake of efficiency, some factories have in place systems that increase productivity but make people unfulfilled and miserable in their jobs.

- For the sake of efficiency, some companies have experimented with requiring hourly employees to be on call even when they are not scheduled to work. This allows companies to minimize excess work capacity without the risk of being caught short-handed, which is financially efficient, but it disregards the workers' quality of life. It requires people to scramble for childcare at the last minute and makes it hard for them to have a second job.

- A rising Gross Domestic Product (GDP) number is used by politicians, economists, and newscasters as a sign that a country is running

---

3. Ibid., 6.

efficiently and thus prospering economically, but it tells us nothing about how real people are experiencing their relationships, whether they are finding meaning in life, or whether all members of a society have enough to feed their children.

Efficiency strives to take precedence over people. Efficiency, when set loose to govern an economic system, becomes a capricious god that strives for wealth accumulation and concentration. It takes on a life of its own and compels people to serve it (this is what Max Weber called the "iron cage of rationality"—we become prisoners of a system that we ourselves have produced). Covenant relationships are of no interest to the gods of efficiency. More work. Fewer resources. No concern for human flourishing. This was Pharaoh's empire-building system. It was a system rejected by the God of Israel.

Israel's God, the God who formed humans on the sixth day of creation and rested on the seventh day of creation, is the God who gave the Israelites a day of Sabbath rest as a sign of a covenant relationship. Sabbath is explicitly *un*productive. Sabbath time offends the gods of efficiency.

Sabbath is a sign that the God of Israel values people in terms of their intrinsic worth, as beings created in God's image, and not in terms of their productive capacity. Sabbath reminds us that we are not defined by how efficiently we produce for a wealth-generating machine. It is a day when we pattern our lives after our God who also rested, rather than after the Egyptian gods who were perpetually restless and demanded the same of their subjects. As Brueggemann asserts, "The conclusion affirmed by the narrative is that wherever YHWH governs as an alternative to Pharaoh, there the restfulness of YHWH effectively counters the restless anxiety of Pharaoh."[4] Sabbath is a day that is deeply concerned with human flourishing rather than human production.

Sabbath continues to challenge us today to view others as intrinsically valuable creations of God, not fundamentally as tools of production. The ethical implications are several. Some of us are in positions to directly make workplace decisions that take the holistic well-being of people as a higher value than economic gain. Others of us are called to influence our bosses and employers to treat people fairly and to compensate them justly rather than coveting profit maximization regardless of human cost. Others of us are protestors; the ethical call for us is to prophetically denounce sweatshop labor or legislation that favors wealth accumulation by the few over the

---

4. Ibid., xiii.

flourishing of all. Sabbath keepers are reminded every week that we are to view one another as created in the image of our merciful and redeeming God. We are intrinsically valuable and freely loved. God does not define us in terms of our productive capacity, and neither should we.

Social Stratification

A second ethical dimension of Sabbath is that it calls us to transcend the stratified categories into which society places people. The fourth commandment specifically names who is to benefit from Sabbath rest. It applies not just to the older members of the community who are in good standing. In the hierarchical culture of that day, as in many cultures still today, the older generation had privileges not granted to the younger generation. This is fine and well to an extent, but the respect granted to those who are older should not feel like slavery to their children. God says that their sons and daughters, too, are to be given rest on the Sabbath (Exod 20:10).

To look out in this way for one's own children may not be that difficult, but to extend Sabbath rest beyond the family may take more resolve. This is exactly what the fourth commandment calls for. Sabbath rest is to be extended not only to sons and daughters, but it is to reach beyond blood relatives to also include those who serve the household (slaves in that context). In our day and age these might be food workers, house cleaners, or gardeners—anyone who does work on our behalf so that we can work less. They deserve and are in need of Sabbath rest as well. Our rest must not be predicated on the labor of others. In God's economy, *everyone* has a day to rest, not just those who are privileged. The scope of the Sabbath command transcends class lines. In this way Sabbath has an equalizing dimension.

The Sabbath challenge to social stratification extends to gender as well. In the patriarchal context of ancient Israel, God specifically states that the females in the community are to be included in Sabbath rest, not just males: "Do not do any work on it—not you, your sons or daughters, your male or female servants" (Exod 20:10). So everyone within the normal flow of community life is included: family, those who serve the family, male and female.

But that's still not all. Any foreigner who happens to be in the community, any "immigrant who is living with you" (v. 10), is to be given the day off also. The Israelites, who knew first-hand what it meant to suffer as a minority population, are not to turn around and treat others in the same way. People of all ethnic groups or nationalities are to be included in the community's Sabbath rest.

The equality of the day is highlighted in the explanation that all these people are to be granted a Sabbath so that they "can rest just like you" (Deut 5:14). What is good for you is good for them. The reasoning embodies the words Jesus reiterates centuries later: "You will love your neighbor as yourself" (Mark 12:31). All are invited to rest in the same way on this day, regardless of their societal labels. The other is like you. As you rest, so should the other be allowed to rest.

Samuel Dresner comments on this idea that Sabbath overcomes social stratification:

> Although one Jew may have peddled onions and another may have owned great forests of lumber, on the Sabbath all were equal . . . . The uneven divisions of society were leveled with the setting of the sun. On the Sabbath there was neither banker nor clerk, neither farmer nor hired-hand, neither mistress nor maid, neither rich nor poor.[5]

With the start of Sabbath, a royal dignity is recognized in each and every person, a dignity that is obscured in the culture of social stratification that dominates the other six days for now.

The expansive scope of the Sabbath command is paralleled remarkably in the language used by the Apostle Paul in his letter to the Galatians. In that letter Paul writes that "there is neither Jew nor Greek; there is neither slave nor free; nor is there male and female, for you are all one in Christ Jesus" (3:28). These are three of the four categories of people noted in the Sabbath commandment! In Christ, the logic of Sabbath equality is reiterated.

As Christians, we are drawn into this same theme every time we celebrate the Lord's supper. At the table of the Lord, we are all equal and all worldly divisions are to be cast aside. Paul takes the Corinthian Christians to task precisely because they failed to do this when they gathered for the Lord's supper. They were forming factions among themselves based on economic status: the "haves" were eating their fill while the "have-nots" were going hungry (1 Cor 11:18–21). Paul doesn't mince words in condemning this abuse of the Lord's supper: "you show contempt for the church of

---

5. Dresner, *Sabbath*, 43.

God and humiliate those who have nothing" (1 Cor 11:22, NRSV). When we partake of the Lord's supper, we are to celebrate as equals the power of Christ's death and resurrection. We recognize at the table the equality that shines forth in Sabbath.

The ethical implication for us is to work toward this sort of Sabbath equality in the broader society. We should work for things like fair lending policies and fair hiring practices that do not discriminate based on age, race, gender, or any other scheme of social stratification. If we allow God to form us through the practice of Sabbath keeping, we will come to care deeply about advocating for the equality embedded in Sabbath.

A Theology of Enough

Our oldest son had a typical teenage-boy's appetite. The amount of food he could consume was partly a result of his involvement in athletics, partly a result of teenage physiological factors, and partly a result of teenage show-manship. On occasion, when he asked to order the monster-sized burger or asked for another helping of food, I would respond, "Does your body *need* it?" I didn't ask the question to save money on groceries or because I feared that he'd become overweight. My hope behind the question was to foster in him a sense of enough. I'm not opposed to the occasional eating contest at summer camp, but in general I would rather not encourage or celebrate another's ability to consume voraciously. One aspect of being a Sabbath people is for us to know when we have enough, to foster within ourselves a spirit of contentment.

God sought to form in the Israelites this spirit of contentment after they left Egypt and were wandering in the desert. In response to their complaining to Moses, God made a plan to provide them with food daily as described in the manna story (Exod 16). Each morning when the dew lifted, the people would now find manna on the ground, and each evening they would be provided with quail for meat.

The arrangement had two stipulations. First, each household was to gather as much as it needed for one day, but not any more than that. If they gathered more than they needed for one day, the next morning the extra manna would be crawling with worms. Second, stipulation number one was suspended on the sixth day. On that day, each household was to gather enough for two days' meals. The seventh day then was to be observed as a holy Sabbath to the Lord, and no manna would appear on the ground on the seventh day. But the extra manna from day six would not spoil on day seven, so the Israelites would still have enough to eat. The God who delivered them from slavery in Egypt would continue to provide for their sustenance. They were not to hoard or hide away more than they needed. They were to be satisfied with enough for the day. They were to live with a spirit of contentment and gratitude for God's provisions.

The stance against hoarding embedded in Sabbath finds expression in a parable Jesus told about a rich landowner whose fields produced so abundantly that the landowner had no place to store the harvest (Luke 12:13–21). His solution was to tear down his old barns and to build bigger ones (remember Pharaoh's storehouses?). The landowner then said to himself, "You have stored up plenty of goods, enough for several years. Take it easy! Eat, drink, and enjoy yourself" (v. 19). The parable goes on to condemn this man. Why? For hoarding. He was hoarding food while others went hungry. He had not learned the Sabbath sensibility of enough.

As it did with the Israelites, Sabbath seeks to shape in us a spirit of contentment and gratitude. In keeping this day, we are challenged not to consume or hold back for ourselves more than we need. This is an ethical issue in terms of our own individual choices, but it is also an ethical issue on a societal level.

While we find contentment and give thanks for the daily bread God has given us, we are called to a holy discontent with a global system in which many do *not* have their basic needs met, and we refuse to accept the world as it is to be the world as it should be. Rather than accepting a society that focuses on accumulating and hoarding, we should pursue a society marked by generosity and compassion. Such a world is all the more possible when we have a sense of what constitutes enough—enough food, enough possessions, enough entertainment, enough power, enough of all the things Americans use disproportionately while each day almost one billion of our brothers and sisters globally do not have enough to eat. Probing the depths of Sabbath should lead us as Christians to see the ethical imperative to act on this issue.

The Haves and the Have-Nots

The justice dimension of Sabbath becomes even clearer as we look at the scriptural teachings on the Sabbath (sabbatical) year given to the Israelites (Exod 23:10–11; Deut 15:1–18). In imitation of the weekly Sabbath, every seventh year was to be a whole year of rest during which the farm land was to remain unplowed. Additionally, during each Sabbath year debts were to be canceled and those who were enslaved—whether because of their own bad choices or because of catastrophic circumstances beyond their control—were to be set free and given another chance. The Israelites were warned against trying to game the system: anyone who wouldn't lend to their needy neighbors as the Sabbath year drew near (thus avoiding a situation where they might not get repaid) would incur guilt for doing so (Deut 15:9).

This system did not eliminate the ability to make a profit and it did not re-distribute all wealth in equal amounts, but it did put in check the accumulation of wealth by some at the expense of others. It didn't allow the Monopoly-game dynamic—where the rich get richer and the poor get poorer—to play out perpetually in real life.

After seven cycles of Sabbath years (forty-nine years), the cycle of Sabbath years was crowned on the fiftieth year with the year of Jubilee. The instructions for the year of Jubilee were similar to those for the Sabbath years, with one major addition. When the Israelites had entered the Promised Land, the land had been divided up between the tribes, and then between the families within those tribes in order to provide all the people with the means to have their needs met (Josh 13–21). In time, some people, whether because of their own ineptitude or because of circumstances such as crop failure, ended up having to sell their land. In that agrarian context, land was the means of productivity and flourishing. Without land, one could not grow crops to feed one's family or to sell or barter for other goods.

As with money, land tends to become concentrated in the hands of the wealthy, so those who had money were able to buy land from the poor and thus increase their already-superior productive capacities. The year of Jubilee contained a provision that addressed this situation. Every Jubilee year all the land was to be given back to the original owners. Those who had lost their land during the course of the previous forty-nine years were given a new opportunity. They were given back the land so that they could again produce crops and raise livestock. They received an opportunity again for full participation in the local economy.

Jesus located himself smack dab in the middle of this Jubilee tradition. In announcing the launch of his ministry in Luke 4, Jesus chose to read a text from Isaiah that has the year of Jubilee as its backdrop: Jesus said that he came to announce good news to the poor, to set the oppressed free, and to proclaim the year of the Lord's favor (Luke 4:18–19). The original year of Jubilee was indeed a sign of God's favor upon the downtrodden. Jesus now introduces a vision for a time of Jubilee that will have no end.

In our day, the biblical theme of Jubilee was the backdrop for a movement that emerged at the turn of the millennium called Jubilee 2000. Bono, lead singer in the rock band U2, has been the best-known face of the campaign, which continues in various forms today. The movement seeks to get the staggering debts of the most impoverished countries in the world cancelled by the wealthy countries that hold that debt. Many of the debtor countries borrowed huge amounts of money at high interest rates in the seventies, eighties, and nineties. The loan system was rife with problems. Some wealthy countries made loans as a way to buy support in the Cold War. Some wealthy countries pushed developing countries to borrow for ill-advised infrastructure projects. Loans were made to corrupt governments whose people never saw the benefits of the money. And some lending countries and organizations required the borrowing countries to implement draconian economic policies that maximized the amount of money the lenders would be repaid but devastated local economies. Because of the money required to service the debt, impoverished countries had little money left to provide clean drinking water, basic health care, and adequate nutrition to their own people. The Jubilee debt remission campaign is a concrete way in today's world through which some have sought to live out the ethics of the Jubilee year described in Scripture.

Sabbath years and Jubilee years are concerned with justice. They hold within them a particular understanding of what constitutes fairness when it comes to economic policies and exchange, a fairness that often looks quit different than the fairness established by conventional laws and policies. Buying and selling, profits and loss, are acceptable, but the economic system is not without limits. Today the richest eighty-five people in the world have a combined financial worth equal to the combined wealth of the 3.5 billion people at the bottom of the wealth scale (half the world's population). The principles of Sabbatical and Jubilee proclaim judgment on this sort of wealth concentration when millions die of starvation and the lack of basic health care.

The prophet Isaiah conveyed words from God that sharply rebuked those who carried out business as usual and acted unjustly while pretending to observe the Sabbath:

> Announce to my people their crime,
>> to the house of Jacob their sins.
> They seek me day after day,
>> desiring knowledge of my ways
>> like a nation that acted righteously,
>> that didn't abandon their God.
> They ask me for righteous judgments,
>> wanting to be close to God.
> "Why do we fast and you don't see;
>> why afflict ourselves and you don't notice?"
> Yet on your fast day you do whatever you want,
>> and oppress all your workers.
> —ISAIAH 58:1b–3

The people here are condemned for their fake piety that neglects justice. In contrast to their hypocritical fasting, God desires something else:

> Isn't this the fast I choose:
>> releasing wicked restraints, untying the ropes of a yoke,
>> setting free the mistreated,
>> and breaking every yoke?
> Isn't it sharing your bread with the hungry
>> and bringing the homeless poor into your house,
>> covering the naked when you see them,
>> and not hiding from your own family?
> Then your light will break out like the dawn,
>> and you will be healed quickly.
> —ISAIAH 58:6–8

This righteous way of living is then connected directly to Sabbath. Or to put it another way, the way they live the Sabbath determines whether or not they are living out God's justice:

> If you stop trampling the Sabbath,
>> stop doing whatever you want on my holy day,
>> and consider the Sabbath a delight,
>> sacred to the Lord, honored,
>> and honor it instead of doing things your way,
>> seeking what you want and doing business as usual,

then you will take delight in the Lord.

I will let you ride on the heights of the earth;

I will sustain you with the heritage of your ancestor Jacob.

The mouth of the Lord has spoken.

—ISAIAH 58:13–14

When was the last time you heard someone connect freeing the oppressed, feeding the hungry, housing the homeless, and clothing the naked with weekly Sabbath observance? Isaiah saw a connection. By pondering these words from Isaiah—the prophet whom Jesus quoted more than any other, we might come to see the connection more clearly ourselves.

Follow the arc forward to our weekly Sabbaths today. Every seventh day we are reminded to let our families, our employees, and all of creation rest. We are reminded that we have an ethical calling, exemplified in Sabbath years and Jubilee years, to act on behalf of our brothers and sisters around the globe and right here at home who are not yet able to experience the fullness of Sabbath provision, rest, and joy. We can never enter the fullest Sabbath rest until all our brothers and sisters around the world are able to rest as well. Until then, our rest is provisional.

Discussion Questions

1. Reflect on idea that while efficiency can be beneficial, efficiency has repeatedly become the taskmaster of oppressive economic systems, a harsh slave driver that brutalizes people. Do you relate to this perspective? Why or why not?

2. How have you seen Christians working to address the issues of inequality and injustice in this country or around the globe? What opportunities do *you* have to address these issues?

3. Describe a business decision or piece of government legislation that has in some way positively addressed the ethical issues connected here to Sabbath.

4. Do you accept the argument that Sabbath ethics call for wealth to be distributed differently than it is now? If so, how would you propose bringing that about?

5. How do you feel after considering these justice issues that are connected to Sabbath keeping? Overwhelmed? Motivated? Indifferent? Angry? Something else?

❧ SLOWING DOWN
Sabbath and Creation Care

> The Acadian flycatcher, not
> a spectacular bird, not a great
> singer, is seen only when
> alertly watched for. His call
> is hardly a song—
> a two-syllable squeak you hear
> only when you listen for it.
> His back is the color of a leaf
> in shadow, his belly that
> of a leaf in light. He is here
> when the leaves are here, belonging
> as the leaves belong, is gone when
> they go. His is the voice
> of this deep place among
> the tiers of summer foliage
> where three streams come together.
> You sit and listen to the voice
> of the water, and then you hear
> the voice of the bird. He is saying
> to his mate, to himself, to whoever
> may want to know: "I'm here!"

—WENDELL BERRY, "SABBATHS 2002: POEM IV"[1]

Like the Acadian flycatcher in this poem, all of creation whispers or shouts in one way or another, "I'm here!" Marvel at what God has made! Have eyes to see and ears to listen! God's good creation calls out to be

---

1. Berry, *Given*, 108. Copyright ©2005 by Wendell Berry, from *Given*. Reprinted by permission of Counterpoint.

noticed. The more we notice all that God has created around us, the more we will come to care for what God has made. Sabbath moves us in this direction of noticing and adds its voice to the biblical call for us to care for all creation.

The earth-care theme started at the beginning of time. In the beginning, after God created the water, the earth, and all living things, Adam and Eve were given responsibility to watch over the fish of the sea, the birds of the air, and the animals on the land. All that was created was declared to be good, and God wanted all these good things to be looked after.

God's care for all creation appears again in the Noah story. When God sent the rainbow, God said to Noah, "This is the symbol of the covenant that I have set up between me and all creatures on earth" (Gen 9:17). The covenant was not just between God and humans. God included "every living being of all the earth's creatures" in the covenant (Gen 9:16).

This creation-care theme emerges in Sabbath as well. Scripture teaches that Sabbath has implications not just for humans, but also for animals and the land. The Sabbath commandment stated that even one's livestock was to be given rest on this day (Exod 20:10). And then, mirroring the seventh day Sabbath pattern, the land was to be given a Sabbath rest every seventh year (Exod 23:10–11; Lev 25:1–7). No crops were to be planted during the Sabbath year, nor were vineyards to be pruned for production. The poor were to be allowed to eat whatever crops self-propagated in the fields during that year, and whatever they didn't eat was to be left for the wild animals to eat. People, livestock, land, wild animals. Sabbath has a connection to all of creation.

If all that God has created is good, and if God cares about all that God created, and if we are to align ourselves with what God cares about, then we should care about creation! Sabbath helps us to see this. As Norman Wirzba puts it, "There is an inexorable logic at work in the Sabbath that will not allow us to separate ourselves from the rest of creation and the creation from God."[2] We are part of the earth's web of life, and what we do can nurture or harm that web. Call it what you will—earth care, creation care, conservationism, environmentalism—we are to pay attention to all of God's creation and to be gentle with it.

In the farming context of ancient Israel, paying attention to the created order might have been a fairly natural thing to do. Farmers pay attention to the arrival of spring to know when to plant. They pay attention to

2. Wirzba, *Living the Sabbath*, 145.

how much rain falls. They pay attention to the nutrients in the soil. They pay attention to the ripening of crops to know when to begin the harvest.

But farmers make up only one percent of the United States population today. For most of us, life has been packaged in such a way that we are not required to pay attention to the created order on a daily basis. We can ignore where our food comes from. We can ignore how clean water gets to the faucet in our kitchen. We can ignore how our driving habits and other consuming activities relate to the created order. We can ignore the major environmental issues of our day. We don't have to pay attention to the created order if we don't want to. But we *should* pay attention if we want to honor God, care for our neighbors, and act as good stewards of all that God has made.

> "Since creation is God's love made manifest and concrete—in the forms of birth and growth, decomposition and fertility, respiration and digestion, healing and vitality—insofar as we are cut off from creation we are significantly cut off from God's action in the world."
>
> Norman Wirzba, *Living the Sabbath*[3]

Sabbath calls us to remember that God is the one who created this world. Sabbath calls for all of creation to rest and be refreshed. Sabbath invites us to slow down and notice God's creation all around us. In Sabbath, we have time to notice that the plant in the pot outside the front door has started to bloom. We have time to notice the intricate beauty of a spider's web that has appeared on the side fence. We have time to notice that the basil seeds planted in the garden have failed to sprout, or that the penstemon plants in the yard are dying for some reason. We have time to notice that the leaves of the trees are changing from the bright green of spring to the deeper green of summer. We have time to notice the incredible beauty in people, who hold a special place in God's created order. When we step into Sabbath time, we have time to slow down and notice. This is but a first step, but it is a step that leads in the direction of caring well for the world entrusted to us.

If I make my Sabbath observance primarily about me, then I have misunderstood Sabbath. The day is first about honoring God, and then about blessing all of creation, which includes you and me, but extends much further. When we realize this, then every seventh day is a celebration of God's creation and a reminder of our role in caring for it.

---

3. Ibid., 143.

The Acadian flycatcher is not a spectacular bird nor a great singer. But he says to his mate, himself, to whoever may want to know: "I'm here!" Listen—all of creation calls out for our attention!

Group Meditation

1. Read aloud Lev 25:1–7.

2. Reflect silently on these verses for several minutes.

3. What stood out for you in this passage? How might these verses intersect with your life today?

five

SABBATH AND CONSUMERISM
Prophetic Confrontation

My friend Mark and I were standing in line at Walmart watching the two boys who were on their own in front of us. The older brother looked to be around thirteen years old, the younger brother maybe nine or ten. They waited as the cashier rang up for them a new school backpack and a few school supplies. From the available clues, I guessed that they were from an immigrant family and that their parents probably worked hourly jobs in the local tourist industry.

When the cashier told them the total amount, they unfolded some bills and counted up some coins. They were a few dollars short. In the split second that followed, as the boys glanced at each other, my friend Mark, who didn't have his wallet with him, whispered to me, "Cover it, Rob." I immediately took a step forward, handed the cashier some bills, and paid for the rest of their purchase. The boys thanked me and went on their way.

Someone else behind us in line said to me, "That was generous. Thanks for doing that." It *was* generous—on the part of my friend Mark. He was the one who saw the need and responded instantly out of a generous heart. It didn't matter that he was being generous with my money (after all, it was only a few dollars). What he saw was a couple of young boys who probably didn't get many breaks in life, a couple of boys who weren't born into the privileges that many take for granted, a couple of boys who just wanted a plain backpack for one of them to take to school like all the rest of the kids. And Mark responded with an uncalculated generosity. I long for that kind of generous spirit.

This is not the kind of spirit nurtured by the forces of Consumerism that dominate our culture today. The monster of Consumerism produces a spirit of selfish desire rather than a spirit of generosity. It generates a spirit of accumulation rather than a spirit of kindness and care for others. It requires our ever-increasing appetites for things and experiences in order for it to survive. If our desire for a more generous spirit is authentic, if we really want a generosity that spills out of hearts overflowing with thanksgiving for what God has done and is doing, then we have no choice but to confront the powers of Consumerism. Otherwise Consumerism will have its way with us. Sabbath takes on the complementary tasks of freeing us from the tentacles of Consumerism and freeing us *for* a counter-cultural way of living as followers of Christ.

During some of my childhood years I lived in North and South Dakota, where "blue laws" were still widely in effect. These laws, which used to be found nationwide, required most businesses to be closed on Sundays. You couldn't shop for clothes, groceries, or household supplies on Sundays even if you wanted to. While most blue laws in the United States have been repealed in the last few decades, remnants remain. Several states still prohibit the sale of alcohol on Sundays. In New Jersey, auto dealers are still forbidden by law from opening on Sundays. In North Dakota, stores may now open on Sundays, but not until after 12:00 noon.

I'm not interested in campaigning to bring back blue laws. My purpose in bringing up these examples is to reflect on the motivation for creating these laws in the first place. If we push back far enough for their origins, we arrive at the

---

Sabbath Experiment Preview

Try stepping out of the economic system for twenty-four hours!

- Don't make any purchases, whether with a credit card, cash, or gift card.
  - » Plan meals in advance and buy the necessary groceries in advance—don't spend money on eating out on this day.
  - » Fill up your car with gas before Sunday.
  - » Don't pay any bills.
  - » Skip Starbucks for the day—brew your coffee at home.
- Don't make *plans* for buying—don't browse for products online or in stores to purchase later.
- Don't balance your checkbook or check your bank statements.
- Do nothing related to earning money.
- Nurture a spirit of thanksgiving for all the ways God generously provides!

ancient Judeo-Christian conviction that earning money and spending money should cease on the Sabbath. Putting aside work and keeping the day holy has meant embracing a sort of time in which commerce comes to a stop. What the broader society has forgotten, the church might do well to remember. It's a move that prophetically confronts the Consumerism of our day.

Consumerism is a powerful and deceptive cultural force because it hijacks the basic human need to consume. We all need to consume food and water to live. Additionally, we need to consume materials for clothing, housing, and so forth. Consuming is required for life. Consumerism, though, is a force that pushes us to consume far beyond our basic needs and redefines what consuming should mean for us. It is a force that promises personal satisfaction from attaining things and status. It is a force that seeks to make us eternally discontent with what we have. It tells us that we will be happier and more satisfied with life if we have the newest cell phone, the new and improved coffeemaker, a bigger and higher-resolution flat screen TV, or the latest high-tech rain jacket for outdoor adventures.

The desire for things is not unique to our day and age. We know that it was an issue for the ancient Israelites because God addresses it in the tenth commandments: don't covet anything that belongs to your neighbor. We see the desire to accumulate expressed in King Solomon's opulent lifestyle. We hear Jesus challenge the value of these desires when he instructs his disciples not to store up treasures on earth.

The ways in which these desires are formed and expressed shifts from age to age and culture to culture. In today's dominant culture, these desires are formed and expressed in relation to the forces of Consumerism.

Consumerism is a force that subtly but insistently promises to satisfy our longings, bless our relationships, and make us lovable. Consumerism is keenly concerned with cultivating our desires because our desires are its lifeblood. Consumerism is a god that needs to cultivate and feed on our desires for the sake of its own survival. Let's take a look at the types of desires that Consumerism generates. Then we'll look at how Sabbath keeping prophetically confronts them and witnesses to an alternative way of forming and living out our desires in light of the Gospel.

Desire to Accumulate

What do you do if you don't have enough room for all your stuff—old furniture, clothing that no longer fits, unused sports equipment, seasonal decorations, and so forth? If you're like one in ten US households, you rent a self-storage unit. The self-storage industry started in the 1960s and has burgeoned since then. The United States currently has about 2.3 billion square feet of self-storage space, which works out to 7.3 square feet of storage space for every single one of the 317 million men, women, and children who live in the United States.[1] We store a lot of stuff.

Sometimes we store things for nostalgic reasons, like boxes of photographs from the pre-digital age or sports trophies belonging to children who long ago grew up and moved out of the house. Sometimes we store things out of convenience. It can be more convenient to stack boxes of clothing, picture frames, old stereo equipment, and children's toys in a storage unit rather than expending the energy to figure out what to sell or give away. Sometimes we store things because we have the notion that they might be useful at some point down the road.

Oliver James, a psychologist and author of *Affluenza*, suggests yet another reason for why we store so many things. He believes that Consumerism has led us to confuse who we are with what we have. To get rid of something, then, means losing a bit of oneself, and James asks rhetorically, "You wouldn't want to throw yourself away would you?"[2] If James is right, and I think there's truth in what he says, then the explosive growth of the self-storage industry is an indication of how our possessions have become extensions of our identities.

Undoubtedly, good reasons exist for storing some items, but the booming self storage industry points to a desire for accumulation that far exceeds such reasons. The forces of Consumerism have led many of us to believe that we will feel better about ourselves and our lives by having more stuff, some of which then needs to be stored. Undergirding the self storage industry is a Consumerist culture that seeks to create in us the desire to accumulate.

---

1. From the Self Storage Association Fact Sheet
2. Cited in de Castella and Dailey, "Self-Storage Craze."

Desire for the New, the Bigger, the Better

After our third child was born, we bought a tent big enough for two adults and three variously-sized kids to sleep in on family camping trips. It was a good tent—easy to set up, durable, and spacious. A couple years later, my brother and his family bought the new version of that same tent, and I learned that this new version had a couple minor improvements, like the way in which the tent doors were stored when unzipped. I wanted the new version. Let me highlight two facts: 1) our tent was still in excellent condition, and 2) we almost never want to keep the tent doors open because this lets in bugs. But still—the way the doors were stored when open on the newer tent was so cool! I didn't need it, but I wanted it. Whether it is a new cell phone, a new bicycle, a new car, or a new microwave, Consumerism persuades us to believe that newer is better—and better enough that we should buy it.

Bigger is also better, right? A couple years ago, our local air quality control district had a program where you could bring in a gas lawnmower (a big source of air pollution where we live) and get a steep discount on an electric mower. When I arrived at the exchange site, I learned that I could choose from two electric mowers: a less expensive one with a smaller battery designed for smaller yards, and a more expensive one with enough battery capacity to mow a larger yard on a single charge. Our yard isn't big, and I calculated that the smaller lawnmower would be more than adequate for our needs. But as I talked to the worker at the exchange site, he strongly suggested that I go with the larger one and I began to wonder if I should indeed pay a bit more to get the bigger mower—just in case. After all, bigger is better, right? A bigger hamburger, a bigger hard drive on your computer, a bigger TV screen, a bigger selection of channels, a bigger ice cooler, a bigger house. Get the biggest size you can afford. With little regard for need, Consumerism tells us that bigger is indeed better. It's all part of the shaping of desire, something at which Consumerism excels.

Desire for an Image

Let me lay out for you three imaginary car commercials. Which car would you want?

Car commercial #1: a nerd pulls up to a stoplight in his new car. In the car next to him are four hot babes jamming to ear-splitting music. The two closest sexy young ladies immediately hang out of the car windows and start flirting with the nerd because of the car he is driving. In fact, because he is driving this car, he is no longer a nerd. His image has changed. The message: you too can turn from a nerd into a chick magnate if you drive this car. (Sexist, gender targeting of this ad duly noted.)

Car commercial #2: an athletic-looking couple leans back against the front hood of their rugged SUV near the edge of a cliff and gazes over the spectacular red-rock canyon country of Utah. The message: people who drive this SUV are adventurous and love the outdoors. You might never leave the urban jungle, but no worries—you too can have the image of an adventurous outdoor-lover if you drive this vehicle.

Car commercial #3: an elegantly dressed couple steps out of a posh restaurant just as the valet pulls up to the curb with their luxury sedan. Once seated in the car, the man and woman are sealed off from the noise of the outside world and cocooned by soft leather seats, crystal-clear sound from the high-end stereo, and exotic-wood interior trim. Then with in-credible smoothness and power, the car accelerates off into the night. The message: you too can have the image of wealth and exclusivity if you drive this car.

Choose the image you desire: sexy, rugged, or rich. Buy the car. Attain the image. The same dynamic can be in play when it comes to designer handbags, the latest fad in basketball shoes, the places we vacation, and the schools to which we send our kids—all can be leveraged for image creation. Consumerism thrives on our desires for a certain image. It doesn't matter what that image is—we can choose from any on the menu; what matters is that we desire it and will spend money to attain it.

Desire for Love

"Our seemingly insatiable quest for money and material consumption is in fact a quest to fill a void in our lives created by a lack of love," claims David Korten.[3] The forces of Consumerism agree with Korten, but reach a dramatically different solution. Consumerism claims that the love void will be filled if money and things are attained. Korten insists that these means will *not* help us find the love we desire. They only compound the distance and emptiness between us. It's a rebuttal that I find deeply resonant with

---

3. Korten, *When Corporations Rule,* 239.

the claims of the Gospel. We need to explore how Consumerism taps this desire to be loved, which is perhaps the most fundamental level of desire.

Let's continue with the advertising theme as our tool of discovery. You've seen numerous ads for diet products that show beautiful, ideally proportioned people (at least according to culturally established ideals), clad in skimpy or form-fitting attire, on a beach or in a gym. The ads suggest that if you use this product you too will be sexually appealing.

Unpack that a bit. Why would you want to be more sexually appealing? To be noticed. And why would you want to be noticed? To have more sex? Maybe. But for many, the desire to be noticed (and perhaps the desire for sex, too) is built upon the desire to be loved. To be noticed opens up the possibility of being loved, whereas to go unnoticed means that you are not loved—and maybe not lovable (so the distorted story goes). The real message of the ads is not the surface promise that the product will help you lose five pounds and make you sexier, but a much more powerful promise of relationship, connection, and love. Consumerism is not actually concerned with fulfilling this promise; it simply taps the longing for love in order to increase sales. Not every ad aims to tap this desire for love, but a notable number do.

The human longing for love is summoned in this sampling of actual TV commercials:

- a KFC commercial shows three generations of a family sitting around a dinner table smiling and laughing together while eating fried chicken.

- an Ikea commercial shows a little boy looking over the balcony of his apartment and making eye contact with a little girl on the balcony of the apartment below; soon he is down on her balcony sharing a sandwich.

- a Coca-Cola commercial shows a stable boy encountering the princess in her bedroom at which point a passionate love scene unfolds.

Family connections, friendship connections, romantic connections—we all desire to be loved somehow by someone. This desire is a desire for relationship, and God created us as relational beings. Consumerism taps into this legitimate desire and whispers that the product of the day will help us have this love. It's a promise on which Consumerism can't deliver.

Sabbath Freedom in a Consumerist Culture

Sabbath prophetically confronts the forces of Consumerism and beckons us to a different way of life. It is a way of life in which we are set free from misdirected desires so that we can live more fully as God's children. The Apostle Paul writes, "Christ has set us free for freedom. Therefore, stand firm and don't submit to the bondage of slavery again" (Gal 5:1). As we step away from the sphere of commerce for one day each week, we say no to the enslaving demands of Consumerism. With this choice, each Sunday we stand in defiant resistance and resolutely refuse to again become slaves in Egypt. Sabbath keeping is more than a "no," however. It is also an emphatic "yes!" It is an embodiment of our freedom to say "yes" to following Christ along the path that leads to grateful contentment, generosity, and love.

> *Reflecting on the Sabbath Experiment:*
> **Off-Line**
>
> "The best part of the Sabbath Experiment for me was not partaking in Consumerism. I spend a lot of time shopping online because it is more convenient than going to the store. With the absence of the use of a computer for the day, I did not feel the need to shop and it allowed me to not even think about it, but to enjoy the time with the people around me."
>
> Bruce
> Technology Support
> Professional

Freedom for Grateful Contentment

While Consumerism seeks to generate insatiable desires, Sabbath teaches us that our desires should have limits. Sabbath seeks to generate in us a spirit of contentment. The Israelites in the wilderness were invited by God to go out each morning and to collect as much manna as their families needed for that day, but not more than that. Surprise, surprise, the people didn't listen but collected more than they needed. The result? The leftover manna "became infested with worms and stank" (Exod 16:20). God wanted the Israelites to be content with enough and to trust in God that enough really was enough.

As we curb our desires for material things, we learn to be satisfied with enough. As we say no to buying and selling one day a week, Sabbath seeks to form in us a spirit of thankful contentment. This is the posture that the Apostle Paul embodied, as described in his letter to the Philippian church: "I have learned how to be content in any circumstance. I know the experience of being in need and of having more than enough; I have learned the secret to being content in any and every circumstance, whether full or hungry or whether having plenty or being poor" (Phil 4:11–12). If we desire to learn like Paul to be content, Sabbath can serve as our teacher.

If a person were to say no to the use of money on Sundays, these are the types of Sunday challenges that will provide practice in contentment:

- the urge to jump online and buy a birthday gift that is already late
- the urge, before the inventory runs low, to buy a pair of running shoes that went on sale today
- the urge to call back the car salesman to take the deal that yesterday he said would expire by the end of the weekend
- the urge to buy concert tickets that just went on sale
- the urge to bid on an eBay item when you remember that the bidding is set to end before the day is out

For the person who has chosen not to use money on Sunday, each contrary urge can be an opportunity to grow in contentment by asking:

- Why might it feel compelling or urgent for me to use money in this way today?
- What might this urge say about my relationship to money and things?
- What is opened up to me by my choice not to accommodate this urge?
- How might God be seeking to form me through this practice for the other six days of the week?

To process at this depth every single urge to spend money, even if only for one day a week, could be fatally exhausting. But to never ask these questions could also be fatal. Perhaps we just do our best to process these questions in fits and spurts as we seek to enter into the rest that Sabbath offers. And we embrace God's grace as the context for both our wrestling and our rest.

A word of warning must be clearly stated: these spending choices are not markers of whether or not God loves you, whether or not you're a real Christian, or your level of moral superiority. To use any aspect of Sabbath to judge or condemn is a misuse of the gift and is implementing a legalism that Jesus rejected. Rather, I suggest that these choices are best seen as expressions of a spiritual discipline. Engagement in the discipline does not earn merit or guarantee an outcome. We engage in spiritual disciplines because we, along with those who have come before us, have experienced them as beneficial to the Spirit-led process of growing in our love for God, love for others, and all the manifestations of this love. These challenges are a means to a greater goal as opposed to being a rigid checklist for doing Sabbath "right." I don't in fact think that there is any one way to do Sabbath "right."

Freedom to be Generous

When we live with grateful contentment, we are free to be generous in ways we are not free when we're mired in impulsive or unconsidered acts of using money. Grateful contentment allows for joyful generosity. It is a generosity that reflects the very nature of our triune God, who generously entered history for our sakes, who generously sent the Spirit, and who generously cares for us in ongoing ways. It is a generosity lived out in the early church following the outpouring of the Spirit on Pentecost:

> All who believed were together and had all things in common; they would sell their possessions and goods and distribute the proceeds to all, as any had need. Day by day, as they spent much time together in the temple, they broke bread at home and ate their food with glad and *generous hearts*, praising God and having the goodwill of all the people. And day by day the Lord added to their number those who were being saved. (Acts 2:44–47 NRSV; italics mine).

In the Acts community, generosity flourished. Members of the Acts community sold their possessions in order to have money to give away. We see here that generosity is more than an attitude. It unfolds in concrete actions. Generous people are freed from attachment to possessions and so are free to lend out their possessions, free to give away food and clothing to those in need, free to financially support causes aligned with God's love and justice, and free to focus on people rather than things.

Freedom for Christ-Shaped Love

By prophetically confronting Consumerism, Sabbath sets us free to love well. As we deconstruct Consumerism's message about possessions, image, and relationships, we come to see the hollowness of it all. We come to see that we will not attain love by the means Consumerism supplies. Nor should we love others based on the criteria Consumerism offers. We put aside the temptation to love others because of their wealth and possessions. We put aside the temptation to love others because of their image or status. As we do so, we are opened to love others as Christ has loved us.

This is a sacrificial love, a love that is willing to give up rights and demands for the sake of the other rather than a love motivated by personal benefit. When our love is shaped by Christ, we seek to love others because of their intrinsic worth as creations of God, rather than because of the extrinsic measures of worth offered by Consumerism. When our love is shaped by Christ, we remain steadfast and desire reconciliation when conflict erupts in a relationship, rather than quickly writing off the other person and looking for more immediate gratification. Christ-shaped love gives, forgives, initiates, blesses. Through its confrontation with Consumerism, Sabbath invites us to say yes to Christ-shaped love.

Sabbath's invitation to step away from accumulating and spending money opens time for loving in this way. When a Sunday is not filled with earning and spending, time is set free for other ways of living. We have taken one option off the table that competes with other ways of relating to our families and friends. Being together in a type of time where money is set aside does not guarantee that we will love others well, but it does help to create the conditions for a love that delights in others, that sees the beauty and wonder within others, and that nurtures communal well-being.

I'm not suggesting that we can draw a short, straight line from the choice to not shop for a new shirt on Sunday to the freedom to love others as Christ loves us. That would be a rather simplistic claim, and we all know that life isn't that simple. It is difficult to guarantee the precise impact of any given choice. However, the accumulation of our choices over time does form us, for better or for worse. The connection between confronting Consumerism and living in Sabbath freedom may take time to see and experience, but in time it will show itself to be real.

Sona and Rafi own the coffee shop where I am sitting this morning as I write. Rafi comes in by 6 a.m. to open the shop and Sona comes in by mid-morning to join him in the work. The two of them handle all aspects of the shop, as business is not brisk enough to have other employees. I have come to know Sona and Rafi as people deeply committed to their Christian faith. This faith led them to make the decision a few years ago to stop opening the coffee shop on Sundays. I'm sure that this little coffee shop does not generate a large income, and so closing for one day a week is significant financially, especially with a son in college. But when Sona told me of the new hours, she mentioned nothing of the financial hardships that might be involved. She simply expressed their desire to do what they felt called to do, and she expressed faith that God would continue to provide for their needs.

Such a choice is only possible when the desires urged along by Consumerism are not allowed to rule. Sona didn't use erudite phrases like Sabbath as confrontation with Consumerism, Sabbath spirituality, or Sabbath rhythms of life. Yet all of these ideas permeate the choice Sona and Rafi made. I see in these two people a love of God, a friendliness with people, a generosity, and a contentment that makes their choice unsurprising. I find it inspiring in its mundaneness. Nothing flashy. No sophisticated intellectual underpinnings. But a faith-guided choice to form a life around God's gift of Sabbath rather than around the incessant demands of Consumerism. It's a choice that recognizes Sabbath as a gift from God, a gift intended to set us free.

Time to Take the Sabbath Experiment Challenge!

1. Begin by looking at "Getting Ready for the Sabbath Experiment!" in Appendix 1.

2. Then read through "The Sabbath Experiment: Guidelines for the Day" in Appendix 2.

3. Pick an upcoming day on which you will try the Sabbath Experiment. Invite others to do this with you on the same day.

4. For this challenge, try to stick to all the Sabbath Experiment guidelines provided, even though you will likely choose a different combination of guidelines for yourself long-term.

5. Schedule a time to meet with others who also did the Sabbath Experiment to discuss how each of you experienced various aspects of the day, using the Sabbath Experiment debriefing questions at the end of chapter 6.

Discussion Questions

1. In what was said about the desires nurtured by Consumerism, were there points that especially resonated with your personal experience or with what you've seen in the broader culture?

2. If stepping away from earning and spending money would be a new Sabbath practice for you, what might be the hardest things for you to change in order to live into this? What do you find inviting about this idea?

3. Going out to eat at a restaurant after church is a common practice for many Christians.

   a. How would you make a case that this is a good exception to the idea of not using money on the Sabbath?

   b. How would you make the opposite case: that this exception to the use of money on Sundays should not be made and other alternatives should be embraced instead?

   c. How do you feel about the idea that there may not be one right answer on this issue?

✑ SLOWING DOWN

Jesus and Sabbath

What did Jesus think of Sabbath? When Christians scan their memories on this topic, the number one search result is usually these words Jesus spoke: "The Sabbath was created for humans; humans weren't created for the Sabbath" (Mark 2:27). This verse is found in the context of a conflict between Jesus and the Pharisees. On one Sabbath, Jesus and his disciples are walking by a wheat field and pause to pick some heads of wheat to eat. This gets them in trouble. They don't get in trouble for stealing—the Law explicitly permitted people to help themselves to a little bit of grain from someone else's field (Deut 23:25). What they get in trouble for is picking grain on the *Sabbath*. Picking a few heads of wheat for a snack was an action that fell under the broader category of harvesting, and harvesting was forbidden on the Sabbath (Exod 34:21). This is the basis for the Pharisees' confrontation.

Jesus responds by referencing David, who also violated the official rules on holiness to feed himself and his followers. David entered a sanctuary and took the consecrated bread to feed his men (1 Sam 21:1–6). Jesus sets his actions in parallel with David's. Then after giving the example of David, Jesus speaks the words about Sabbath being created for us, not us for the Sabbath.

Sometimes these words have been taken to mean that Sabbath no longer matters, but Jesus' response could not have meant, "ignore the Sabbath," because Jesus himself observed the Sabbath regularly. For example, Mark tells us that "Jesus and his followers went into Capernaum. Immediately on the Sabbath Jesus entered the synagogue and started teaching" (Mark 1:21). We read in numerous other places too about Jesus going to the synagogue on the Sabbath. He was an observant Jew and his attendance and teaching in the synagogue were part of regular Sabbath observance.

In his confrontation over picking grain on the Sabbath, Jesus was not abolishing Sabbath but was challenging the way it had come to be understood and practiced. The day was never intended to rule over people. Rather, the day was intended to serve people by connecting them to God.

The role of Sabbath was in a sense to watch over the covenantal relationship between God and God's people. It was never intended to police alleged petty offenses.

We get further insight into Jesus' view of Sabbath through his involvement in five Sabbath healing stories recorded in Luke's gospel.[1] In one of these stories, the scribes and Pharisees use Sabbath as part of their ploy to discredit and get rid of Jesus (Luke 6:6–11). As Jesus enters the synagogue to teach on a Sabbath (here again, we see Jesus' regular Sabbath observance), he encounters a man whose hand is crippled. The scribes and Pharisees know that Jesus is in the healing business, and they see an opportunity: if they can catch Jesus healing on the Sabbath, they can bring charges against him because they equated healing with work.

Jesus knows their game and uses it to his advantage. Aware that he is being watched, he calls the man over to him. Then before he heals the man's hand, Jesus turns to the scribes and Pharisees and says, "Here's a question for you: Is it legal on the Sabbath to do good or to do evil, to save life or to destroy it?" (Luke 6:9). They don't answer him. The trap is sprung, but it is the scribes and Pharisees who are caught in it, not Jesus. The answer to the question, obvious to all, is that it is lawful to do good. And who is going to argue that healing a man's crippled hand is not a good thing to do? Jesus then proceeds to heal the man's hand, much to the chagrin of the religious authorities (v. 11).

In two other healing passages Jesus continues to challenge the religious leaders regarding what is acceptable to do on the Sabbath. He reminds them that they are willing to lead their livestock to water on the Sabbath (Luke 13:15) and are willing to pull a child or an ox out of a well on the Sabbath (Luke 14:5). The upshot of both passages is this: if you are willing to care for those other physical needs on the Sabbath, then certainly attending to the physical need of healing is also acceptable on this day.

The Jewish people saw the weekly Sabbath as a time that foreshadowed the final reign of God. They anticipated that all the themes of the weekly Sabbath would emerge forevermore when God's kingdom came in full. They understood that future reign to be a time when the lame would walk, the blind would see, the sick would be cured, and the hungry would be fed.

---

1. These five Sabbath stories are found in Luke 4:31–37; 4:38–41; 6:6–11; 13:10–17; and 14:1–6.

In light of this, it is not accidental that Jesus' Sabbath violations fall into two categories: healing and feeding. He is creating the conditions that correlate with God's reign! Jesus is doing something more here than challenging a legalistic view of Sabbath; Jesus is making the astounding proclamation that through his actions the kingdom of God has arrived and an eternal Sabbath is unfolding! This correlates with Jesus' inaugural announcement of his mission in which he identifies himself as the fulfillment of the year of Jubilee (Luke 4:18–19)—as we saw earlier, the year of Jubilee is through and through a Sabbath event.

Jesus did indeed challenge the views of Sabbath held by the Pharisees and others, but beyond pushing against their legalism, he was proclaiming that the eternal Sabbath was at hand. N. T. Wright claims, "the sabbath was the regular signpost pointing forward to God's promised future, *and Jesus was announcing that the future to which the signpost had been pointing had now arrived in the present.*"[2] Rather than casting off Sabbath, Jesus was living it in full.

Group Meditation

1. Read aloud Luke 6:6–11.

2. Reflect silently on these verses for several minutes.

3. What stood out for you in this passage? How might these verses intersect with your life today?

---

2. Wright, *Simply Jesus,* 137.

six

SABBATH AND THE SELF
The Storms That Rage Within

> Six days a week we seek to dominate the world,
> on the seventh day we try to dominate the self.
> —ABRAHAM JOSHUA HESCHEL, *THE SABBATH*[1]

For all its beauty, for all its embodiment of delight, joy, celebration, relationships, and grace, Sabbath can also lead into darkness and struggle. In the stillness of Sabbath rest, sometimes we become aware of the previously obscured turbulence from the storms that rage within. As we come to see more clearly through Sabbath the way God intends things to be, we may also come to see more clearly that we ourselves are not yet aligned with God's intentions, or even our own. To face this reality can be deeply painful and disturbing.

When Elijah sought the voice of the Lord, first the deafening noise all around him had to cease. The event is recorded like this: "A very strong wind tore through the mountains and broke apart the stones before the Lord. But the Lord wasn't in the wind. After the wind, there was an earthquake. But the Lord wasn't in the earthquake. After the earthquake, there was a fire. But the Lord wasn't in the fire. After the fire, there was a sound. Thin. Quiet." (1 Kings 19:11–12). It was in the quiet that Elijah heard the voice of God, and often this is where we, too, may hear God in new and different ways. But sometimes we calm the external deafening noise only to become acutely aware of the deafening noise within. Issues and anxieties that are easy to ignore or obscure amidst the noise and hubbub of daily living become difficult or impossible to avoid in the revealing stillness of

---

1. Heschel, *Sabbath*, 13.

Sabbath. They make it impossible to hear "a sound of sheer silence" (1 Kings 19:12, NRSV). As overwhelming and uncomfortable as it can be, we must face these issues if we are going to enter fully into Sabbath rest.

Control

Sabbath keeping reveals to us the limits to our control. When we cease striving for a day, we are reminded that our Creator God, the God who created the mountains and the plains, the sky and the oceans, and the flora and fauna, is the One who is ultimately in control. God is the one who keeps the world spinning in its orbit, God is the one from whom all good things come, and God is the one who will usher in the fullness of the Kingdom. Sabbath reminds us that God is in control and we are not. Sabbath reminds us that ultimately all our strivings for control are limited. While we can control some elements of our lives to some degree, much of life is beyond our control.

Yet the struggle to control is rooted deeply within us. We want to control our relationships and our homes. We want to control our work environments and our futures. The types of things we try to control include:

- the image others have of us
- the way a loved one responds to a statement or situation
- the friends our children choose
- the lifestyle standard we will have in retirement
- the alphabetical organization of the kitchen spice drawer (or more generally, the feel of our living space, whether organized or not)
- the way we age
- the theological particulars of our church

Attention to detail and organization can be one manifestation of control—an attempt to account for and control all the variables in one's life so that things don't feel out of control. Ironically the carefree spirit unconcerned with detail or organization can also be a manifestation of control. For some, the choice to not care is a method of controlling what is able to hurt them or what is able to overwhelm them. The carefree spirit can be a method of control through rejecting the authority claims of others. The penchant to control comes in many forms.

Then is everything out of our control? I am not a fatalist. I don't think that every detail of life just happens to us in a manner that transcends our choices and involvement. God calls us to steward this earth, to love, and to serve. All these suggest that we have some degree of control over how we live our lives and the choices we make. However, this truth is too quickly confused with the delusion of complete or ultimate control. When we live under such a delusion, we are playing God.

In our Sabbath observance, God seeks to give us perspective on our control. We are shown that when we rest for one day a week, the world keeps moving. It is not, in fact, our efforts that control its rotations. And we are shown that despite our most gallant efforts, we can't hold it all together all the time. We must come to terms with our limitations. We must come to terms with the fact that we are finite beings. As we cease striving to control, we are released to more fully worship the God who is able to work in ways above and beyond what we could ever imagine or achieve (Eph 3:20). We trust control to this God.

> *Reflecting on the Sabbath Experiment:*
> **Desire for Control**
>
> *"The Sabbath experiment highlighted a few things about myself that could be considered 'idols' in my life. First, I realized how much control I like to have of my time and schedule. Letting go of control of tasks was extremely difficult for me. I have a hard time not working and I know that is a result of me not giving God enough credit for what God has done, is doing, and will do. I stack up my responsibilities so high that I'm afraid if I stop they'll all come tumbling down. I know that I need to prioritize, not take on too much, and be okay with not being the savior of everything."*
>
> *Maressa*
> *Pastor*

While Sabbath rest gives us time to reflect on these issues of control, our chosen Sabbath structures often lead us to experience of the limits of our control as well. At least this has been my experience. I can control some aspects of my Sabbath observance—I can control for the most part whether or not I get the house cleaned by supper time on Saturday night, whether I go to worship with our church family on Sunday morning, and whether I set aside my work for the day. But my ideals for Sabbath transcend my control. I often fail on Sunday to connect with my wife and children as I desire—sometimes because I don't initiate (which I can control), but sometimes despite my best efforts to spend time together. I can't control that connection. Sometimes my Sunday is characterized less by the joy and celebration of the day and more by feelings of dissatisfaction, unease, and restlessness. Try as I might, I cannot control the mood of the day, for reasons within as well as for reasons without. Coming face to face in Sabbath time with my desire to control and my inability to control increases my awareness of how this issue of control plays out during the rest of the week, too. At times this is deeply troubling. The storms rage within.

Compulsions

Some people are blessed with the ability to easily let go and to relax without distraction. Others, though, find this more difficult. In the stillness of Sabbath, their compulsions emerge, and again the storms within begin to rage. If you identify with this second group of people, perhaps you relate to one of these:

- the compulsion to accomplish something
- the compulsion to surround oneself with sound
- the compulsion to immediately read and respond to text messages
- the compulsion to eat
- the compulsion to prepare
- the compulsion to clean or organize
- the compulsion to be entertained

The calmness of Sabbath peace gives way to sinister dark clouds, thunder, and lighting. An awareness of one's compulsions and attempts to resist them can set loose the internal storms' full power.

This awareness piles struggles upon struggles as we realize how our compulsions are played out during the other six days of the week too. One person realizes that she has turned away from a hurting friend during the previous week because of a compulsion to stay on task. Another realizes that he waited too long to tuck his child into bed because of a compulsion to finish a project on the computer, and the child fell asleep alone. Yet another realizes that while at the coffee shop with his friends he was obsessing about an issue at work and so really has no idea what his friends said or how they're doing. Awareness. Conviction. Turmoil. The storms rage within. Am I willing to face these raging forces? Or will I seek to outrun them and settle for a shallow peace?

Reflecting on the Sabbath Experiment:

A Horrible Feeling

"With the candle lit and the food on the table, we ate and talked and enjoyed that the TV was off, if only for the novelty of it being so silent. After dinner we played and wrestled with the kids on the living room floor. At this point, the Sabbath Experiment was fun and interesting.

After we put the kids to bed, we realized how odd it felt to have no TV to watch or computers to use to sift the internet looking for entertainment. At first I didn't know what to do with myself. I have taught myself to relax while hopping from channel to channel and conversing with my wife about whatever we were watching. Without the option of TV or computers, we chatted for a bit, I played my guitar for a few minutes and we went to bed earlier than we normally would have.

The odd feeling of not knowing what to do with my time because I am so comfortable watching TV was a horrible feeling."

Buzzy
Senior Pastor

Boredom

Sabbath is sometimes boring. Many of us are accustomed to filling our lives with tasks and entertainment. I want to accomplish things on my never-ending to-do list, because accomplishing things makes me feel good. I want to relax—or numb out—by flipping on the TV or surfing the internet. When I put aside these urges, what am I left with? Sometimes the answer is boredom.

Our culture communicates to us that boredom should be avoided at all cost. If active engagement or participation is too much work, just sit back and passively take in what is offered on the ever-expanding menu. Entertainment, shopping, listening to music—anything to push out boredom. The message for young and old alike: you deserve to never be bored.

While boredom is not enjoyable, are we in fact better off by never experiencing it? What might be revealed if we are willing to look inside when the feeling of boredom arises? Boredom raises these questions:

- What are the things I use to fill my life so that I am not bored? Are these the things I want to shape my values, my relationships, and my sense of the Holy?

- What ideas of meaning and purpose bother me when I am bored, and why do I feel scared, overwhelmed, and insignificant when these big life questions creep up out of the abyss?

- Why is it that I am bored rather than content?

Such questions can lead to a place of darkness within, a place of troubled waters. I'm all for feel-good Sabbaths, but sometimes Sabbath is a place of dryness where the feelings of contentment, joy, and connection evaporate.

If we experience Sabbath as boring, have we failed? I think not. The focus of Sabbath transcends our feelings. In fact, if we make feelings our focus, then we have taken the primary focus off God. As Marva Dawn notes in relation to Sabbath, frustration with emotional dryness "exposes the fault that we are focusing on our feelings instead of on what God is like in all God's all-consuming grace and love!"[2] God created us as emotional beings and emotions are an important aspect of the spiritual journey, but they are not an adequate guide in and of themselves for how we make choices regarding our spiritual formation, nor are they an adequate measure of our spiritual lives. If we embrace patterns of spiritual formation only as long as they make us feel good, our spiritual maturity will certainly be stunted.

> *Reflecting on the Sabbath Experiment:*
> **Filling Time**
>
> *"I personally struggled with feeling lazy. Just sitting and doing nothing made me realize all the things that could be done. Crazy things, like fixing the cabinets in our garage or giving our dog a bath came to mind. I was looking for anything to fill the time and help me be productive. Instead I paid attention to my son."*
> Brian
> *Pastor of Media and Communications*

The restlessness of boredom sometimes stems from a lack of patience. I can be impatient with rest. I can be impatient for Sabbath to end. I can be impatient to get at the work that lies before me in the week ahead. I can be impatient that I have not shaped my living environment into the place I want it to be. I can be impatient that our children do not live each Sabbath according to my expectations. I want to step out of rest to work on these

---

2. Dawn, *Sense of the Call*, 78.

things. Everything in its time says the writer of Ecclesiastes, but I often do not want to wait for the right time. I can be impatient. It takes much training to embrace this time for what it is, to live in this moment rather than to live with a restlessness about another moment, whether in the future or in the past. Despite the biblical teaching that patience is a virtue with which we are to clothe ourselves (Col 3:12), I do not always want to embrace it. Sabbath keeping sometimes reveals this darkness within.

Relational Void

The stillness of Sabbath can be a lonely place. The invitation of the day to celebrate with others can reveal the absence of relationships. The prayers to begin Sabbath have parts for different people. The evening meal that starts the Sabbath is a feast to be eaten with others. The singing, game playing, and conversations that make for a celebratory Sabbath are communal events. But what if one does not have a community? What if such relationships, even if longed for, are missing?

When it raises these questions, Sabbath can lead to a place of pain and loneliness. Pain from love lost or love never found. Pain from isolation. Loneliness from living in a new place where friendships have not yet formed. If the time comes when others are not available or willing to participate with me in Sabbath observance—then what?

Sometimes the issue lies within. The Sabbath vision makes me long for points of relational connection on a Sunday afternoon: a conversation, a walk, playing a game together, *something*—but sometimes I pull back from the effort it would take to draw others in. Inertia is more powerful. It is easier not to initiate. And so I slip back into isolation. In that isolation I become aware of my inability to love others as I want. I become aware that I love others on my terms and expect them to respond on my terms. It raises questions about what else in me keeps me from opening up to relationships with others. What life choices do I make that communicate that friendships are low on my priority list? And what in me makes it hard for others to be with me? In opposition to the joy toward which Sabbath bends, a darkness can arise, an awareness that I myself am a block to Sabbath joy.

Perhaps the isolation is really no fault of my own. The reality is that sometimes circumstances isolate. As was the case for Job, sometimes a person does the right things, but isolation still comes. Then what? This can lead to another level of despair. Crying out to God. Why me? I don't deserve this—I have been a good kid, I've done what you asked. Why this? And maybe there is a shift from crying out to God to wondering if there even is a God. How could there even be a God if my best efforts are ignored and my impassioned prayers do not bring the connections I so long for? I'm not asking for material things—I'm asking for relationships. This isn't selfish is it? Doesn't the Christian faith claim that we are created for relationships? If there is a God who created people for relationships, then why would such a God not provide them when I genuinely seek them? We're now a long way from a Sabbath of smiling faces, happy time with loved ones, and joyful refreshment.

Facing Idols

Keeping the Sabbath can also make us keenly aware of the idols in our lives. The Ten Commandments include an injunction against idolatry: "You must have no other gods before me. Do not make an idol for yourself—no form whatsoever—of anything in the sky above or on the earth below or in the waters under the earth. Do not bow down to them or worship them " (Exod 20:3–5a). I don't know of any Christians in our cultural context who are tempted to worship little carved figurines in their homes, but often idols are present nonetheless. Idolatry goes beyond worshipping specific gods like Baal or Ashera. Idolatry extends to forces or activities to which we show excessive loyalty as evidenced by our servitude to them. The apostle Paul describes greed as a form of idolatry (Col 3:5). Greed certainly continues to be an idol for many today; what else might qualify? Sometimes our idols can be identified by reflecting on what pulls us away from Sabbath rest.

> *Reflecting on the Sabbath Experiment:*
> **The Idol of Busyness**
>
> *"I realized that I was not even trusting God to contain and sustain my life for one twenty-four hour period. I initially wanted to present a justification for my attempts to control my life but soon relented to the good news that I was, after all, not in charge. Busyness and my small accomplishments had become my 'idol' and, like all idols, was replacing God. This was not a new realization; I had confronted this idol many times in the past, but the centrality and power of this drive to busyness was brought home to me with fresh clarity in the Sabbath Experiment."*
>
> Robin
> Retired Psychiatric
> Social Worker

I hate to say this because I'm a sports fan, but in our culture a common form of idolatry involves sports. When schedules are routinely re-worked around sports events, when family gatherings, church activities, and friends' significant milestones are made second-tier priorities beneath sports, when attending sports practices or sports events trumps all else, the god of sports wins. Allegiance is misplaced.

Youth Sports and the Sabbath

One day, in a car conversation with our oldest son about my work on this book, I reflected on the seriousness with which Sabbath was set forth for the Israelites in the Hebrew Scripture: the punishment for not observing Sabbath was the death penalty (Exod 34–35). And I wondered about how that might inform participation in sports games and practices on Sundays today. I was a bit taken aback by his response: "Why didn't you just say no to Sunday games and practices?" In that moment, it seemed so simple: just say no.

But at other times it seemed anything but simple. For years we chose to allow our daughter to play organized soccer, and often games were scheduled on Sundays. So some configuration of our family would often miss our church community's worship service during the soccer season. We did it because of the joy and physical outlet it provided for our daughter, and we felt that we didn't need to be legalistic about Sabbath. Also, I really enjoyed watching her play, and that enjoyment seemed consistent with Sabbath themes. And saying no to these games might have caused the parent-child relationship to take a pretty big hit. I'm fairly comfortable with the choices we made, yet in my Ideal Sabbath Picture, league games would not take place on Sunday mornings, or on Sundays at all. Sometimes I wonder what it would have been like if we had indeed just said no.

When faced with this situation, one option is to go to a Saturday night worship service or to do a small family worship service at some point before or after the game on Sunday so that worship is still a part of the Sabbath. Also, numerous other elements of Sabbath are not ruled out by Sunday games, so they can still be thoughtfully integrated into the day.

Some will react strongly against this sharp language. The retort goes like this: "Watching sports can be a healthy form of relaxation, and participating in sports can be healthy for our bodies." Points granted. Sports can be wonderfully subsumed in Christian faith, as can technology and a range of other forces. But what is it again that constitutes idolatry? It is allowing a force to make a claim on our allegiance that competes with our allegiance to the One True God. How do we tell the strength of an allegiance? By the daily and weekly ways we pattern our lives in relation to a given force; by the ways we allow it to form us.

Once again we see that the rest offered by Sabbath can be not only disrupted but also disrupting. By revealing our idols, Sabbath can cause great struggle. It's not all fun and games. To free ourselves from idolatry requires a counter-cultural steely determination, the companionship of traveling partners, and the breath of the Holy Spirit upon us.

Jesus Calms the Storms

The storms that rage within do not have the last word. Sabbath can not only stir up, but can also be a means of calming the storms. The psalmist offers praise to the God who "leads me beside still waters" (Ps 23:2, NRSV). Jesus brought still waters when a raging storm on the Sea of Galilee threatened to sink the disciples' boat: he "gave orders to the winds and the lake, and there was a great calm" (Matt 8:26). The God who leads beside still waters, the God who calms the seas, is the God who can calm the storms within as well. It may be that we can only arrive at that state of being by looking deep within and acknowledging the troubled waters. Sabbath provides a context and prompting for this difficult work.

> "Having made peace with the conflicts that rage *about* us—both with nature, of whose true Lord Sabbath observance teaches us, and with society, of whose true purpose Sabbath rest makes us aware—it is easier for us to make peace with the strife that burns *within* us."
>
> Samuel Dresner, *The Sabbath*[3]

3. Dresner, *Sabbath*, 51–52.

Discussion Questions

1. To what extent and in what contexts is the desire to control an issue for you?

2. Are there times when you have experienced silence as troubling, anxiety-producing, or uncomfortable? Are there times when you have experienced silence as peaceful, holy, or refreshing? Describe them.

3. To what extent have you experienced Sabbath as boring? What do you make of this?

4. What else does Sabbath stir deep within you?

Debriefing the Sabbath Experiment!

If you took the Sabbath Experiment challenge put forth at the end of chapter five, use these questions to discuss what that experience was like for you.

1. What feelings came up for you in connection with the Sabbath Experiment?

2. What was hard about this? Why?

3. What were the best parts of this for you?

4. Which elements of the Sabbath Experiment could you envision embracing over the long term?

⇀ SLOWING DOWN

More New Testament Connections

Like Jesus, the apostle Paul maintained the practice of Sabbath observance. We are told that when Paul and Barnabas arrived in Antioch, they kept the Sabbath by going to the synagogue (Acts 13:14). And we are told that in Thessalonica, "As was Paul's custom, he entered the synagogue and for three Sabbaths interacted with them on the basis of the scriptures" (Acts 17:2). It was his custom to keep the Sabbath.

Yet Paul understood clearly that Jesus had ushered in a new covenant, and that had implications for Sabbath keeping. Paul argues that for those who are in Christ, religious practices must not serve as a means of judgment. Paul puts it this way: because of what Christ has done, "don't let anyone judge you about eating or drinking or about a festival, a new moon observance, or sabbaths" (Col 2:16). Keeping food purity laws and adhering to a sacred calendar are not requirements for those who have been set free by the work of Christ. Like Jesus, Paul both kept the Sabbath and sought to re-frame it.

Another important New Testament reference to the Sabbath is found in the book of Hebrews. The author of Hebrews uses Sabbath language to describe the type of rest into which the faithful enter. After a discussion of who enters into this rest and who doesn't, the author writes, "So you see that a sabbath rest is left open for God's people. The one who entered God's rest also rested from his works, just as God rested from his own" (Heb 4:9–10). Sabbath rest here is a theological motif, not a direct instruction for concrete practices. But for the motif to be most fully understood, the actual experience of Sabbath rest must be part of the readers' lives.

Beyond specific references to Sabbath, we find numerous thematic connections to Sabbath throughout the New Testament. Here I will highlight three. One is the theme of rest, which comes through in Jesus' promise of rest to those who are exhausted, overwhelmed, or beaten down. Jesus says, "Come to me, all you who are struggling hard and carrying heavy loads, and I will give you rest. Put on my yoke, and learn from me. I'm gentle and humble. And you will find rest for yourselves. My yoke is easy to bear, and my burden is light" (Matt 11:28–30). Walter Brueggemann helps us make the connection to Sabbath:

> "Weariness, being heavy-laden, yoke" are all ways of speaking of the commodity society of endless productivity. In context, this might have referred to the strenuous taxation system of the Roman Empire, for "yoke" often refers to imperial imposition. Alternatively, this may have referred to the endless requirements of an over-coded religious system that required endless attentiveness. With reference to imperial imposition or over-coded religion, Jesus offers an alternative: come to me and rest! He becomes the embodiment of Sabbath rest for those who are no longer defined by and committed to the system of productiveness. In this role he is, as he is characteristically, fully in sync with the tradition of Israel and with the Sabbath God who occupies that tradition.[1]

This Sabbath theme of rest is a word of grace. Christ invites us into the same rest that God graciously offered the Israelites when God delivered them from slavery in Egypt.

A second Sabbath theme is that of loyalty to God. One place this shows up in the New Testament is in the Sermon on the Mount where Jesus says, "No one can serve two masters. Either you will hate the one and love the other, or you will be loyal to the one and have contempt for the other. You cannot serve God and wealth" (Matt 6:24). Note the clear parallel to the first of the Ten Commandments: "You shall have no other gods before me" (Exod 20:3; NRSV). God wants our undivided loyalty.

Brueggemann again helps us make the connection to Sabbath: "The way of *mammon* (capital, wealth) is the way of commodity that is the way of endless desire, endless productivity, and endless restlessness without any Sabbath. Jesus taught his disciples that they could not have it both ways."[2] Undivided loyalty to God leaves behind the restless system of mammon and leads to Sabbath rest. Sabbath is an embodiment of such loyalty.

A third Sabbath theme carried forward in the New Testament is that of trust. Continuing on in the Sermon on the Mount, Jesus says to those listening, "Don't worry about your life, what you'll eat or what you'll drink, or about your body, what you'll wear" (Matt 6:25). He says further that God

---

1. Brueggemann, *Sabbath as Resistance*, 11–12.
2. Ibid., 11.

cares for the birds of the air and the lilies of the field and so will certainly care for people as well. Don't worry. Trust God.

Worry is what the Israelites did in the desert after they were freed from slavery in Egypt. In response, God promised to provide sustenance for them. You'll recall that God also gave specific instructions to gather only enough for that day. Would they trust God to provide again the next day or would they try to stockpile extra food? God watched to find out: "In this way, I'll test them to see whether or not they follow my Instruction" (Exod 16:4). This Sabbath theme of trusting in God's generous provisions comes forth clearly in the words of Jesus about not worrying. God cared for the Israelites in the desert, and God cares for the birds of the air and the lilies of the field. Don't worry. Trust. Sabbath living is a demonstration of our trust in God to care for us, too.

The New Testament does not contain the same sort of detailed teachings on Sabbath observance found in the Old Testament. But as we have seen, in specific references to Sabbath as well as in thematic continuity, the New Testament carries forward the invitation to embrace the Sabbath.

Group Meditation

1. Read aloud Matt 6:25–34.

2. Reflect silently on these verses for several minutes.

3. What stood out for you in this passage? How might these verses intersect with your life today?

seven

CONCLUSION
Ideals and Realities

Is Sabbath spirituality actually possible in a 25/8 culture? That depends. If we take as our starting point the urgency, expectations, and values of the dominant culture and then try to add Sabbath to that, then Sabbath keeping may in fact prove impossible today. But that's not the only starting point we have to choose from. A different starting point becomes possible:

- if we decide that Sabbath is indeed a gift so precious that we will go to great lengths to protect and treasure it,

- if we decide that Sabbath observance will indeed help to rightly orient us toward the Creator and creation,

- if we decide that Sabbath is a blessing to our relationships,

- if we decide that the biblical and theological dimensions of Sabbath are so deep and compelling that we want to spend a lifetime exploring them,

- if we decide that Sabbath really does confront consumerism, injustice, technological deformation, and the storms that rage within, and

- if we find the Sabbath melody to be one we can't get out of our minds, a melody we catch ourselves humming here and there throughout the rest of the week.

Sabbath then does indeed become possible today. If we value it, we can learn to observe it, even in today's culture. The truth of this is reiterated in these words from Samuel Dresner:

> Only from the conviction of the value of the Sabbath will there fol-
> low a willingness to keep it. Keeping the Sabbath today demands

sacrifice. When did it not? But the cost is small for so rich a blessing.[1]

Yet even with the best of intentions and convictions, Sabbath will not always unfold as we hope. I have a mental image of my own ideal Sabbath, but the reality is that my Sabbaths often do not match up with this ideal. Let me recount a recent Sabbath experience to show you the tensions and conflicts that commonly impinge upon my Ideal Sabbath Picture.

It was Saturday afternoon and I was finishing up yard work and other tasks in order to be ready to start Sabbath as a family with our evening meal. I had stepped inside for a few minutes when a loud banging on the glass porch door momentarily knocked me out of my anticipation-of-Sabbath-peacefulness mindset. One of our kids had come home, and rather than knocking politely on the locked door and waiting, or going around to the unlocked front door, or using the hidden key less than 10 feet away (obvious choices that any well-raised child would choose from, right?), this child ignored all my previous parental admonitions against doing so and pounded demandingly on the locked glass door to be let in. My internal volcano didn't erupt in full, but it did immediately begin to rumble and spew ash. This wasn't part of my Ideal Sabbath Picture.

By the grace of God I didn't get too stuck in my own issues, and a little while later we were all gathered at the dinner table, ready to join in our Sabbath liturgy before enjoying the Saturday evening meal together. My Ideal Sabbath Picture was still a possibility. Then before the meal had even started, two of our kids got in an argument and one of them stormed off to her room. This wasn't what dinner looked like in my Ideal Sabbath Picture. Fortunately our daughter soon returned, things were smoothed over with her brother, and we all shared a fairly peaceful and pleasant dinner together that adequately corresponded to my Ideal Sabbath Picture.

But as we cleared the table, my wife and I exchanged a few testy words over some now-unremembered slight, and my desire to join in an after-dinner game with the family took a hit. The conflict between my issues and my ideals rumbled for a while before I was swayed to let go and join the others for game night.

Our start of Sabbath on this particular Saturday evening wasn't a total disaster, but it only vaguely resembled my Ideal Sabbath Picture. Was it a

---

1. Dresner, *Sabbath*, 78.

failure? Probably, if the goal is getting Sabbath "right." But part of the goal of Sabbath keeping is to let it form us. By its contrasting character, the Sabbath made the moments of impatience and conflict more vivid, and thus it also made more vivid my need for ongoing transformation.

I came away from that experience more aware that I need to keep growing in patience and grace. I came away more aware that I can't control others—and shouldn't try to. I came away from the experience reminded that Sabbath isn't first and foremost about me. And I came away from it thankful that we could have another go at practicing Sabbath together seven days later. It didn't match up with my Ideal Sabbath Picture, but it did something better than that. It added brush strokes to the Sabbath picture that I hadn't imagined. So, was it a failure? I think not. Not by a long shot.

As we seek to embrace and grow in a Sabbath rhythm of life, we all will have times when our ideals collide with our realities. Rather than feeling discouraged by this, we might instead seek to discern how God is present and moving right in the midst of these collisions. The God who gave us Sabbath is also the God of grace who knows our hopes, our limitations, and our imperfections. Ours is a loving and patient God who will bless our efforts toward faithfulness, however imperfect they may be.

In encouraging people toward embracing Sabbath, Samuel Dresner speaks of a "ladder of observance." He is more concerned that people are standing somewhere on the ladder—observing Sabbath in some way—rather than how high up they are on it. Dresner says this: "some of us may be at the very bottom; others may be several rungs up. What is important is not where we stand on the ladder at the moment, but that we are willing to try to move up rung by rung."[2] It doesn't matter if a person is on the first rung or many rungs up. What matters is the willingness to ascend it. We are all invited to take a step on the ladder of observance.

By now hopefully it is clear that what we do on this one day of the week develops a Sabbath spirituality that ripples outward into the other days of the week as well. Sabbath spirituality really has to do with a whole way of life, not just a twenty-four-hour experience. The training and formation we receive through this one day equips us for living faithfully in the rest of the week too. Through the practice of Sabbath, our relationships during the rest of the week are affected as we more naturally slow down and

---

2. Ibid., 79. Dresner attributes the phrase "ladder of observance" to Abraham Heschel.

become more present with others. We notice more readily during the rest of the week the beauty of creation all around us because our time in the Sabbath vision clinic has helped us to see more clearly. The limits we put on technology during our Sabbaths teach us to master the technology in our lives at other times, too, rather than being mastered by it. We find that during the other days of the week all the compulsions that we set aside on the Sabbath have a little less power over us. The deep commitment to justice and the well-being of others that is formed by the theology of Sabbath causes us to notice those we see during the week who are at the lower end of society's economic and social scale, and we commit ourselves to work for the sort of world in which they, too, have enough and are able to celebrate Sabbath rest along with us. This is Sabbath spirituality for the whole of life.

> "If we are able to feel the power and grandeur and peace of the Sabbath one day a week, learning to mend our tattered souls and join flesh and spirit in joy and rest, in inward feeling and outward act, perhaps we shall be able to bring a portion of the spirit of this day into the other days of the week, so that even the ordinary weekday will take on something of the Sabbath."
>
> Samuel Dresner,
> *The Sabbath*[3]

The final note sounded by Sabbath is that of hope. Each Sabbath for Christians is a mini-Easter, a celebration of Resurrection hope. Each Sabbath is an invitation to be swept up once again into the newness of life made possible by the risen Christ, in whom we find all the themes of Sabbath fulfilled. This Resurrection hope points us to God's kingdom coming, and Sabbath gives us a glimpse of that kingdom. We strain forward toward that day, when all will be made right, when war and hunger will be no more, when reconciliation and justice will be full—when God's restful shalom will come to all the earth. May the light of Sabbath guide us toward that day.

---

3. Ibid., 63.

Blessed are You, O Lord our God, King of the universe,

who has sanctified us by Your commandments,

and commanded us to kindle the Sabbath lights.

May the Sabbath-light which illumines our dwelling

cause peace and happiness to shine in our home.

Bless us, O God, on this holy Sabbath,

and cause Your divine glory to shine upon us.

Enlighten our darkness and guide us and all humankind,

Your children, towards truth and eternal light. Amen.[4]

Discussion Questions

1. What does your Ideal Sabbath Picture look like?

2. How have your ideals and realities collided when it comes to Sabbath observance?

3. If someone unfamiliar with Sabbath were to ask you what Sabbath spirituality is, how would you respond? How is this similar to or different from how you would have responded before reading this book?

4. What might it look like to invite your whole community into Sabbath spirituality? How might you go about it? What might be the challenges? What might be the rewards?

---

4. Adapted slightly from the opening prayer of the traditional Jewish home service for Sabbath eve as found in Dawn, *Keeping*, xvii.

Appendix 1

GETTING READY FOR THE SABBATH EXPERIMENT!

Choosing

For this experiment, choose to begin your Sabbath observance with the evening meal on Saturday night. Saturday night moves easily into celebration and rest because the following morning will not bring with it the pressing demands of regular work days. Many choose to start their Sabbaths on Sunday morning rather than Saturday night, and then make the whole of Sunday evening part of their Sabbath. But it can be difficult to hold onto the Sabbath spirit during the Sunday evening hours as the demands of Monday morning press in. By starting on Saturday night, you can get in a full twenty-four hour Sabbath, end it with the Sunday evening meal, and then start ramping up for the week ahead by catching up on email and attending to other matters for the coming days. So for this experiment, mirror the biblical pattern of the day starting at sundown. You can adjust this to a calendar day later if you wish.

Preparing

Prepare for Sabbath by getting all your shopping done and your living space put in order before the Saturday evening meal. In planning the menu for Saturday evening, prepare an especially favorite dish to highlight the celebratory nature of the time. Choose and put in place symbols to remind you of the different nature of this time into which you are entering—perhaps an arrangement of fresh flowers, pictures of loved ones, or candles.

At least a couple days in advance, invite others to join you for the Saturday evening meal. Even if only members of your household will join in the meal, specifically invite them, until a Sabbath rhythm is developed. A brief explanation of what your guests are being invited to participate in may keep them from being surprised when the time comes for the Sabbath liturgy to be read just before the Saturday evening meal.

Welcoming

Welcome the Sabbath by joining with others in the Sabbath liturgy before your evening meal on Saturday (see the sample Sabbath liturgy in Appendix 3 and download it from www.TheSabbathExperiment.blogspot.com). This liturgy is adapted from one passed on to my family two decades ago by friends of ours, and we still use it today. It contains some parallels to the Kiddush, the traditional Jewish liturgy used to welcome Sabbath. It also includes elements that point to the work of Christ, reflecting its design for use in a specifically Christian context. You might also consider writing your own liturgy for this purpose!

We often have friends present when we do this reading on Saturday evening. Sometimes I'll let them know in advance that we'll be doing our usual Sabbath-welcoming ritual. If these friends are not Christian or if I am unsure of their faith background, I invite them to join in at the points where they feel comfortable but to also feel free to just observe.

Embracing

Embrace the experiment by closely following the specific guidelines in Appendix 2. These guidelines might be rather shocking and disruptive for some, while others will find them to be fairly easy to incorporate. Remember, there is no one right way to observe Sabbath or one mandatory set of guidelines, but for the sake of this experiment, stick to the detailed guidelines provided.

Be sure to choose one thing you will add to or include in your Sabbath that will help it feel like a celebration. Maybe it will be playing music loudly and dancing in the living room, or maybe it will be going for a leisurely walk in a nearby park. Don't skip this part! It is essential to the tone of the day.

If you're married, embrace the rabbinic encouragement to have intercourse on the Sabbath. This is another element of celebration and another way of affirming the goodness of what God has created!

Keep in mind that for future weeks you are encouraged to adjust and to experiment with your own set of guidelines. Some find that a cold-turkey approach works for them. They begin by blocking out on the calendar the twenty-four hours each week designated for Sabbath, and then fill in around that twenty-four hour block with the other commitments for the week.

Some choose to implement immediately all the elements in the provided guidelines, and may even add to them. Depending on your personality, this approach might work well for you.

Another approach is to develop Sabbath patterns more incrementally. This may involve choosing just a couple of the guidelines to incorporate into the rhythm of your Sabbath and to focus on these for the next few weeks or months. Then add another guideline or two. Even after just a year of this, you will have slowly but dramatically re-calibrated the rhythm of your Sabbath days.

Releasing

End your Sabbath day together with a simple meal. After the meal, while giving each person something sweet (like a chocolate chip or a caramel), say something along these lines: "May the sweet taste of Sabbath stay in your mouth all week long." The Sabbath has now come to an end. Savor the blessings of the day. Anticipate its coming again in seven days, when you get to practice once more living the Sabbath in your chosen ways.

Appendix 2

GUIDELINES FOR THE SABBATH EXPERIMENT

(Available for download at www.TheSabbathExperiment.blogspot.com)

WARNING: Potential spiritual health hazard. Do not try this without first understanding the spirit of Sabbath!

For this experiment, Sabbath observance will begin with the evening meal on Saturday and go through the evening meal on Sunday. Please remember that following these guidelines is not the only way to observe the Sabbath. Consider this an experiment from which you may discover additions and deletions that might shape your Sabbath observances.

1. Prepare for the Sabbath
    a. Choose in advance one activity that will help this day be a celebration for you and write it down it here:

        _____

    b. Clean your living space.
    c. Buy all your groceries, gas, and other things on Saturday or earlier.
    d. Invite family and friends that you would like to join with you.

2. Begin your Sabbath with an evening meal on Saturday with family and/or friends.
    a. Light three candles to signify the presence of Christ, remembering the Sabbath (Exod 20:8), and observing the Sabbath (Deut 5:12).
    b. Before the meal, prepare for and read together the Sabbath liturgy provided in Appendix 3. You can download the liturgy from www.TheSabbathExperiment.blogspot.com and then modify it as you wish.
    c. After the meal, spend the rest of the evening doing something fun!

3. Embrace the rest offered by the Sabbath.

    a. Take a nap.

    b. Don't work.

        i. Don't do things for which you earn money.

        ii. Don't clean the house.

        iii. Don't wash your car.

        iv. Don't do laundry.

        v. Don't organize your office/papers/books.

        vi. Don't fix or repair anything.

    c. Married couples are invited to follow the rabbinic encouragement to make love on the Sabbath.

    d. Don't study.

    e. Don't make lists of things to do in the coming week.

4. Worship with your church community.

    a. In preparation, start thinking about this as you begin the Sabbath observance on Saturday night—pray for others in your community who will be coming together on Sunday.

    b. Plan to get to church a few minutes early and stay a few minutes late—build margins into your worship experience for preparation, conversations, and reflection.

5. Choose to opt out for the day from the economic system of buying and selling.

    a. As a conscious way of confronting the idolatries of consumption and materialism, don't use any money or credit cards.

    b. Plan meals at home or in a park with family and friends rather than going out to eat.

    c. Don't pay any bills.

    d. As already mentioned, buy your groceries, gas, etc. on Saturday.

6. Put aside mediated experiences and artificial units of time.

    a. Turn off your cell phone for the day, except to call loved ones.

    b. Keep your TV turned off (so, no movies or sports on TV).

    c. Keep your computer turned off.

        i. Don't look at your email—it will be there waiting for you after the Sunday evening meal.

        ii. Don't surf the internet.

    d. Take off your watch during the worship service, or for the day.

7. End the Sabbath observance with a simple meal.

    a. As part of your prayer before the concluding meal, offer a prayer of thanks for the Sabbath day.

    b. At the end of the meal, give something sweet (like a chocolate chip or a caramel) to each person and as you do so, say something like this: "May the sweet taste of Sabbath stay in your mouth all week long!"

Appendix 3

A CHRISTIAN SABBATH LITURGY
(Available for download at www.TheSabbathExperiment.blogspot.com)

This is a ritual to be used prior to the Saturday evening meal, before the food is brought to the table.[1] *Position three unlit candles in the middle of the table, one to signify Sabbath remembrance (Exod 20:8), one to signify Sabbath observance (Deut 5:12), and one to signify the presence of Christ. Re-assign parts below as appropriate depending on the presence of children and guests.*

Parent 1: Light is the sacrament of God's presence among us. The Lord is our light and our salvation.

Light the candles.

Child 1: We are called to be children of the Light and to be a light to all nations.

Parent 2: May our home be made holy, O God, by Your Light. May the Light of love and truth shine upon us as a blessing from You. Amen.

Parent 1: Let us prepare our hearts to welcome this first day of a new week: Sunday.

Child 2: On this day our Lord Jesus Christ rose from the darkness of the tomb to bring light to the world!

Parent 2: This meal brings blessings to our hearts as our workday thoughts and toils are forgotten.

---

1. Much of this is adapted from Edward M. Hays, *Prayers for the Domestic Church: A Handbook for Worship in the Home* (Notre Dame, IN: Forest of Peace, 2007), 112–13. Part is adapted from the traditional Jewish Kiddush prayer recited before the evening meal at the start of Sabbath. The first response by "All" is adapted from Col 3:12–14 (NIV).

Parent 1: We thank You, God, for the blessings of this past week: for life and for love, for our health, for family and friendships, and for the gifts that have come to us from our labors. *If children are present:* We especially thank You for these young ones whose lives You have entrusted to us and we pause to ask Your blessing upon them. *Starting with the youngest child, parents put their hands on each child's head and offer a blessing. If guests have children present, those parents may be asked in advance if they would like to offer blessings for their children, or one blessing may be said over all the children.*

> *Examples:*

- "Kate, I pray God's richest blessings upon you. May you have the courage of Esther and the devotion of Mary, and may you walk in the ways of Christ all the days of your life. Amen."

- "Greg, I pray God's riches blessings upon you. May you grow in your compassion for those in need, may you grow in kindness to love your friends well, and may you be filled daily with the joy of Christ. Amen."

Parent 2: Blessed are You, Lord God, King of the Universe, who gives us our daily bread and the fruit of the vine. We thank you for this meal that we are about to share.

All: In response to Your generosity, we desire, Lord, as Your chosen people, holy and dearly loved, to clothe ourselves with compassion, kindness, humility, gentleness, and patience. To bear with each other and to forgive whatever grievances we may have against one another. To forgive as You forgive us, and over all these virtues, to put on love, which binds them all together in perfect unity.

Parent 1: Blessed be this home and this table; blessed be this family and all who sit around our table. Blessed be God and blessed be those who live in God's love. Amen.

Child: The peace of the Lord be with you!

All: And also with you! *Each person is encouraged to share the peace of the Lord with every other person present.*

Everyone now helps to bring the food to the table—let the feast begin!

BIBLIOGRAPHY

Adler, Iris. "How Our Digital Devices Are Affecting Our Personal Relationships." *WBUR News*, January 17, 2013. http://www.wbur.org/2013/01/17/digital-lives-i.

Berry, Wendell. *Given: New Poems*. Washington, DC: Shoemaker & Hoard, 2005.

Brueggemann, Walter. *Sabbath as Resistance: Saying No to the Culture of Now*. Louisville, KY: Westminster John Knox, 2014.

Carr, Nicholas G. *The Shallows: What the Internet Is Doing to Our Brains*. New York: W. W. Norton, 2010.

Cramer, Steven C. "Repairing the Human Brain after Stroke: I. Mechanisms of Spontaneous Recovery." *Annals Of Neurology* 63.3 (2008) 272–87.

Croft, Janet B., et al. "Association between Perceived Insufficient Sleep, Frequent Mental Distress, Obesity and Chronic Diseases among US Adults, 2009 Behavioral Risk Factor Surveillance System." *BMC Public Health* 13.1 (2013) 1–8.

Dawn, Marva J. *Keeping the Sabbath Wholly: Ceasing, Resting, Embracing, Feasting*. Grand Rapids: Eerdmans, 1989.

———. *The Sense of the Call: A Sabbath Way of Life for Those Who Serve God, the Church, and the World*. Grand Rapids: Eerdmans, 2006.

de Castella, Tom, and Kate Dailey. "The Self-Storage Craze." *BBC News Magazine*, Sept 1, 2011.

Draganski, Bogdan, et al. "Temporal and Spatial Dynamics of Brain Structure Changes During Extensive Learning." *Journal of Neuroscience* 26.23 (2006) 6314–17.

Dresner, Samuel H. *The Sabbath*. New York: Burning Bush, 1970.

Ferdman, Roberto A. "Crushing It: The American Energy Drink Craze in Two Highly Caffeinated Charts." *Quartz*, March 26, 2014. http://qz.com/192038/the-american-energy-drink-craze-in-two-highly-caffeinated-charts/

Hays, Edward M. *Prayers for the Domestic Church: A Handbook for Worship in the Home*. Notre Dame: Forest of Peace, 2007.

Heschel, Abraham Joshua. *The Sabbath: Its Meaning for Modern Man*. New York: Farrar, Straus and Giroux, 1951.

Immordino-Yang, Mary Helen, et al. "Neural Correlates of Admiration and Compassion." *Proceedings of the National Academy of Sciences of the United States of America* 106.19 (2009) 8021–26.

Jones, Jeffrey M. "In U.S., 40 Percent Get Less Than Recommended Amount of Sleep." *Gallup Poll News Service*, December 19, 2013. http://www.gallup.com/

poll/166553/less-recommended-amount-sleep.aspx?utm_source=sleep&utm_medium=search&utm_campaign=tiles.

Korten, David C. *When Corporations Rule the World.* 2nd ed. San Francisco: Berrett-Koehler/Kumarian, 2001.

Liu, Ziming. "Reading Behavior in the Digital Environment: Changes in Reading Behavior over the Past Ten Years." *Journal of Documentation* 61.6 (2005) 700–12.

Small, Gary W., et al. "Your Brain on Google: Patterns of Cerebral Activation During Internet Searching." *The American Journal Of Geriatric Psychiatry: Official Journal Of The American Association For Geriatric Psychiatry* 17.2 (2009) 116–26.

"Twitter and Facebook Could Harm Moral Values, Scientists Warn." *Telegraph.co.uk*, April 13, 2009. http://www.telegraph.co.uk/news/science/science-news/5149195/Twitter-and-Facebook-could-harm-moral-values-scientists-warn.html.

Weng, Helen Y., et al. "Compassion Training Alters Altruism and Neural Responses to Suffering." *Psychological Science* 24.7 (2013) 1171–80.

Wirzba, Norman. *Living the Sabbath: Discovering the Rhythms of Rest and Delight.* Grand Rapids: Brazos, 2006.

Wright, N. T. *Simply Jesus: Who He Was, What He Did, Why It Matters.* New York: HarperOne, 2011.